Marcus Gardley

The House That Will Not Stand

Bloomsbury Methuen Drama
An imprint of Bloomsbury Publishing Plc

B L O O M S B U R Y
LONDON · NEW DELHI · NEW YORK · SYDNEY

Bloomsbury Methuen Drama
An imprint of Bloomsbury Publishing Plc

Imprint previously known as Methuen Drama

50 Bedford Square
London
WC1B 3DP
UK

1385 Broadway
New York
NY 10018
USA

www.bloomsbury.com

BLOOMSBURY, METHUEN DRAMA and the Diana logo are trademarks of Bloomsbury Publishing Plc

First published 2014
Reprinted 2014

© Marcus Gardley 2014

British Library Cataloguing-in-Publication Data
A catalogue record for this book is available from the British Library

ISBN: PB: 978-1-4742-2884-8
ePDF: 978-1-4742-2885-5
ePUB: 978-1-4742-2887-9

Library of Congress Cataloging-in-Publication Data
A catalog record for this book is available from the Library of Congress

Series: Modern Plays

Typeset by Country Setting, Kingsdown, Kent CT14 8ES
Printed and bound in Great Britain

TRICYCLE THEATRE
A local theatre with an international presence

The Tricycle views the world through a variety of lenses, bringing unheard voices into the mainstream. It presents high quality and innovative work, which provokes debate and emotionally engages. Located in Brent, the most diverse borough in London, the Tricycle is a local venue with an international vision.

The Tricycle Theatre produces world-class British and international theatre that reflects the rich diversity of our local community.

We present theatre that crosses different continents, voices and styles; theatre that tells stories about how human connections are made through differences of culture, race or language.

Recent productions include Moira Buffini's Olivier Award winning *Handbagged*, a satirical drama about the Queen and Margaret Thatcher which transferred to the Vaudeville in the West End; and the multi-award winning *Red Velvet* (Critics' Circle Award, Evening Standard Award), Lolita Chakrabarti's play about the pioneering Black actor, Ira Aldridge, which transferred to St Ann's Warehouse, New York.

International partnerships include *Paper Dolls* by Philip Himberg with Sundance Theatre Lab. Nationally, the Tricycle has recently co-produced with Shared Experience, and collaborated with Tiata Fahodzi, Liverpool Everyman, and Eclipse Theatre.

Our ambitious Creative Learning programme aims to develop the imaginations, aspirations and potential of children and young people. We invest in creating meaningful relationships with young people sometimes described as 'harder to reach' or who are passionate about theatre but have limited access to it.

www.tricycle.co.uk

A WELCOME FROM
THE DIRECTOR

Just over a year ago a close friend sent me a play that they said they knew I would love. As soon as I read *The House That Will Not Stand*, I immediately began working out when I could programme it. I was certain that this was a story I wanted to bring to the Tricycle.

Whilst over in New York for the transfer of *Red Velvet*, I met the playwright Marcus Gardley to discuss the potential of bringing the play to Kilburn. We got on immediately. I could see how his artistic vision matched the Tricycle's and, thankfully, he agreed that we could stage the UK premiere.

Like all good drama, this play is both personal and universal. Marcus has been inspired by his own family's experiences growing up in New Orleans, as well as the historical setting of nineteenth-century Louisiana, within a political context I knew nothing about.

The play is set during a time when extreme prejudice and enforced oppression formed a social hierarchy that was based on gender and skin colour. It continues to be relevant by challenging our perceptions of freedom today.

It has been wonderful to work with this text. After five weeks in a rehearsal room full of laughter and tears, we look forward to sharing this experience with you.

Indhu Rubasingham

Indhu Rubasingham
Artistic Director
Tricycle Theatre

The House That Will Not Stand
by Marcus Gardley

Odette	Ronke Adekoluejo
Agnes	Ayesha Antoine
La Veuve	Michele Austin
Beartrice	Martina Laird
Makeda	Tanya Moodie
Marie	Josephine Clare Perkins
Maude Lynn	Danusia Samal
Monsieur L. Albans	Paul Shelley

Creative Team

Director	Indhu Rubasingham
Designer	Tom Piper
Lighting Designer	Paul Anderson
Composer	Paul Englishby
Sound Designer	Carolyn Downing
Movement Director	Lucy Hinds
Production Manager	Tariq Rifaat
Company Stage Manager	Shannon Foster
Deputy Stage Manager	Charlotte Padgham
Assistant Stage Manager	Imogen Firth
Assistant Director	Harry Mackrill
Set Builder	MBT Productions and Ridiculous Solutions
Chief Electrician	Charlie Hayday
Head of Sound	Mike Thacker
Lighting Board Operator	Ben Jones
Costume Supervisor	Holly White
Head of Wardrobe and Wigs	Sophia Heron
Voice Coach	Richard Ryder
Fight Director	Kevin McCurdy
Illusion Consultant	Darren Lang
Casting Director	Briony Barnett
Press Representation	Kate Morley
Costume Makers	Eve Collins, Wendy Knowles and Rachel Thomas
Hair	Pam Foster
Hire Costumes	Cosprops
Prop Maker	Michalis Kokkoliadis

Tricycle Crew

Andy Furby, Liam Hill, Russell Martin, Devika Ramcharan, Ben Reeves, Sam Stewart, Bob Weatherhead

Thanks to Jenny Jules, Dan Lockett, Alex Caplen and the National Theatre Sound Department , Chris Traves

This production is supported by Jon and NoraLee Sedmak.

THE WRITER

Marcus Gardley

Theatre credits include: *The Gospel of Loving Kindness* (Victory Gardens Theatre, Chicago, nominated for outstanding playwright 2014); *Black Odyssey* (Denver Theater Center, nominated for best play in 2014); *dance of the holy ghosts* (Yale Repertory Theater and Baltimore Center Stage), *On the Levee* (Lincoln Center Theater – nominated for 11 Audelco awards); *Every Tongue Confess* (Arena Stage, Edgerton Foundation New Play Award), *The Road Weeps, The Well Runs Dry* (Los Angeles Theater Center, Pillsbury House Theater, Perseverance Theater and University of South Florida).

Marcus Gardley is the recent 2012 James Baldwin Fellow. He holds the 2011 PEN/Laura Pels International Foundation for Theater Award for a Playwright in Mid-Career and is a Mellon Foundation grantee for a playwriting residency with Victory Gardens in Chicago. His play *every tongue confess* premiered at Arena Stage starring Phylicia Rashad and directed by Kenny Leon. It was nominated for the Harold and Mimi Steinberg/ American Theatre Critics New Play Award, the Charles MacArthur Award for Outstanding New Play, and received the Edgerton Foundation New American Play Award. Other accolades include the 2011 Aetna New Voices Fellowship at Hartford Stage, Helen Merrill Award, a Kellsering Honor, National Alliance for Musical Theatre Award, Eugene O'Neill Memorial Scholarship, and ASCAP Foundation Cole Porter Award.

He holds an Master of Fine Arts in playwriting from Yale Drama School and is a member of Dramatists Guild of America and Lark Play Development Center. Marcus is a professor of theatre and performance studies at Brown University.

THE CAST

Ronke Adekoluejo / *Odette*

Ronke trained at RADA.

For the Tricycle: *The Colby Sisters of Pittsburgh, Pennsylvania.*

Theatre includes: *Anon* (Welsh National Opera); *Random* (Crooked Path).

Theatre whilst in training: *The Seagull, Cockroach, The Grace of Mary Traverse, Women Beware Women.*

Television includes: *Suspects.*

Film includes: *One Crazy Thing*

Ayesha Antoine / *Agnes*

Theatre includes: *We Are Proud to Present...* (Bush Theatre); *Tartuffe* (Birmingham Rep.); *Venice Preserved* (Spectator's Guild); *Absurd Person Singular, Surprises, My Wonderful Day* (Stephen Joseph Theatre/ National Tour/ 59E59 Theatre NYC); *One Monkey Don't Stop No Show* (Sheffield Crucible/Eclipse Theatre tour); *Blue/Orange* (Arcola); *The Mountaintop* (Derby Playhouse); *The 13 Midnight Challenges of Angelus Diablo* (RSC); *Carrot* (Theatre 503); *Madblud, FamilyMan, Cinderella, Red Riding Hood* (Theatre Royal Stratford East); *Big White Fog* (Almeida); *The Firework Maker's Daughter* (Lyric, Hammersmith/Told By An Idiot tour).

Television includes: *Doctor Who, Holby City, Bellamy's People, Mongrels, Mouth to Mouth, Grange Hill, The Bill, Skins, Pompidou.*

Radio includes: *The Case of Mr H, The Aeneid, Richest Man in Britain, Sacred Hearts, No. 1 Ladies Detective* Agency (BBC); *Obla Air* (British Council). Ayesha is currently the voice of Jackfm2 107.9fm.

Ayesha won a TMA award and was nominated for a Drama Desk Award for her performance in *My Wonderful Day*.

Michele Austin / La Veuve

Michele trained at Rose Bruford College.

Theatre includes: *I Know How I Feel About Eve* (Hampstead Theatre); *To Kill A Mockingbird* (Regent's Park Theatre); *Sixty-Six Books* (Bush Theatre); *Generations* (Young Vic); *Out In The Open* (Hampstead Theatre); *The Riots* (Bernie Grant Arts Centre); *50 Revolutions* (Oxford Stage Company), *Our Country's Good* (Out of Joint/Young Vic), *Breath Boom, Been So Long* (Royal Court); *It's A Great Big Shame* (Theatre Royal Stratford East).

Film includes: *Parking Wars, Another Year, The Infidel, I'll Sleep When I'm Dead, Second Nature, All Or Nothing* and *Secrets and Lies.*

Television includes: *The Casual Vacancy, Death in Paradise, Harry and Paul, Holby City, The Bill, Secret Life, Canterbury Tales- Wife of Bath, Ugetme, Doctors, Who Cares, The Last Detective, Clare In The Community, A&E, Casualty, Night and Day, Gimme Gimme Gimme, Comedy Nation, Home and Away, Babes In The Woods, Skank, Kiss Me Kate, Perfect Blue, Frank Stubbs Promotes* and *EastEnders.*

Martina Laird / Beatrice

Theatre includes: *Moon On A Rainbow Shawl, The Five Wives Of Maurice Pinder* (National Theatre); *The White Devil, Troilus and Cressida, Three Hours After Marriage* (RSC); *All the Little Things We Crushed, Liquid Gold* (Almeida); *Breath, Boom* (Royal Court); *Othello* (Donmar Warehouse); *Hopelessly Devoted* (Birmingham Rep); *Inheritance* (Live Theatre); *Bad Blood Blues* (Theatre Royal Stratford East); *Mules* (Young Vic); *Hyacinth Blue* (Lyric Hammersmith).

Television includes: *Casualty Series 16-21* (Winner Michael Elliott Foundation and the BFM Awards), *London's Burning, Shameless, Coronation Street, EastEnders, Doctors, My Family, Missing, Free Agents, Monday Monday, Little Big Mouth, Always And Everyone, Wing And A Prayer, Touch Of Frost; Jonathan Creek; The Knock; The Governor; Little Napoleons; The Bill; Peak Practice; Thief Takers; One For The Road.*

Film includes: *Blitz, Forget-Me-Not, Deadmeat, The Hurting.*

Radio includes: *Vacant Possession, Mandrake, Lamplighter, Mi Cuba, A Midsummer Night's Dream, Minty Alley, Carmina's Island, Radio 121, Buxton Spice.*

Martina was nominated for the Evening Standard Best Actress Award for her performance in *Moon On A Rainbow Shawl* (2012).

Tanya Moodie / Makeda

For the Tricycle: *The Piano Lesson*

Theatre includes: *Intimate Apparel* (Ustinov, Bath/Park Theatre, London); *Fences* (Bath Theatre Royal/West End); *The Under Room, Chair, A Thousand Stars Explode in the Sky* (Lyric Hammersmith); *Catch, AC/DC, Fewer Emergencies, Incomplete and Random Acts of Kindness* (Royal Court); *The Overwhelming, The Darker Face of the Earth, The Oedipus Plays* (National Theatre); *66 Books* (Bush Theatre); *Trade, Peer Gynt, Coriolanus, Measure for Measure* (RSC); *Lysistrata* (Arcola); *A Doll's House, Medea* (West Yorkshire Playhouse); *Much Ado About Nothing* (Salisbury Playhouse); *The Vagina Monologues* (West End/ UK Tour); *Anything Goes* (Grange Park Opera); *The Prince of Homburg* (RSC, Lyric Hammersmith); *The Suit* (Young Vic/world tour); *The School for Scandal* (RSC, Barbican); *As You Like It* (Bristol Old Vic, West Yorkshire Playhouse).

Film includes: *Legacy, Rabbit Fever, The Tulse Luper Suitcases, The Final Passage.*

Television includes: *Dicte, Common, Skins, Sherlock, Lewis, The Body Farm, Holby City, The Street, The Clinic (Series 6 and 7), Casualty, Sea Of Souls, Silent Witness, Richard Is My Boyfriend, Archangel, Shane, Absolute Power, Prime Suspect 6, Promoted to Glory, In Deep, High Stakes, Always & Everyone, The Bill, Dr Willoughby, Maisie Raine, Boyz Unlimited, A Respectable Trade, Neverwhere, So Haunt Me, The Man From Auntie.*

Radio includes: *Poetry Please, The Amen Corner, With Great Pleasure, Small Island.*

Tanya was nominated in the category of Best Actress at the What'sOnStage Awards 2014, for her performance in *Fences*.

Clare Perkins / *Marie Josephine*

Clare trained at Rose Bruford College.

For the Tricycle: *How Long Is Never?*, *Fabulation*.

Theatre includes: *Little Revolution* (Almeida); *How To Be Immortal* (Penny Dreadful UK Tour); *The Rover* (Hampton Court Palace); *Welcome To Thebes* (National Theatre); *The Caucasian Chalk Circle* (Shared Experience); *The Hounding of David Oluwale* (Eclipse/ West Yorkshire Playhouse); *Any Which Way* (Only Connect); *A Fag Burning The Carpet* (King's Head); *Cyrano De Bergerac, Our Country's Good* (Nuffield Theatre, Southampton); *Generations of the Dead* (Young Vic); *Mules* (Royal Court).

Film includes: *7Lives, Blacklands, Deadmeat, Bullet Boy, The Football Factory, Secrets And Lies, Ladybird Ladybird, Hallelujah Anyhow*.

Television includes: *EastEnders* (series regular), *Run, Verbatim Riots, BBC Learning: True Stories, Doctors, Holby City, Casualty, Clapham Junction, Talk To Me, All In The Game, Shoot the Messenger, Family Affairs* (series regular), *The Crouches, Baby Father, Mersey Beat, A&E, My Wonderful Life* (3 series).

Radio Includes: *Westway* (series, 8 years), *Weak At The Top, Brassic, Landfall*.

Clare won the award for Best Actress at the Screen Nation Film and Television Awards, 2005.

Danusia Samal / *Maude Lynn*

Danusia trained at Central School of Speech and Drama

For the Tricycle: *Circles*

Theatre includes: *Billy The Girl* (Soho Theatre); *Finding Noor* (Citizens); *The Birthday Party* (Royal Exchange, Manchester); *1001 Nights, Liar Liar* (Unicorn Theatre); *Seven* (Pleasance London); *After the Rainfall* (Pleasance Edinburgh/ Watford Palace); *Street Scene* (Young Vic), *The Suit* (Joined Up Thinking/ Young Vic).

Television includes: *Boom*

Paul Shelley / *Monsieur L. Albans*

Paul trained at RADA.

Theatre includes: *King Lear* (Theatre Royal, Bath); *The Conquering Hero* (Orange Tree); *Medea, Earthquakes in London* (UK Tour); *Moonlight* (Donmar Warehouse); *A Voyage Round My Father* (Salisbury Playhouse); *Macbeth* (Chichester/ West End/ New York); *The Merchant of Venice, Absurd Person Singular, The Invention of Love, A Man For All Seasons, The Real Thing* (West End); *The Secret Rapture, The Crucible, Hedda Gabler, Lady in The Dark* (National Theatre); *Les Liaisons Dangereuses, The Winter's Tale, The Twin Rivals, Dingo, Bingo* (RSC); *Antony and Cleopatra* (Shakespeare's Globe).

Television includes: *Paradise Postponed, Titmus Regained, A Tale of Two Cities, Morse, Secret Army, The Fourth Arm, Midsomer Murders, Heartbeat, Revelations, Dr Who, Blake's 7*.

Film includes: *Oh! What a Lovely War,* Polanski's *Macbeth,* Rupert Goold's *Macbeth, Caught in the Act, It Shouldn't Happen to a Vet.*

Paul has directed several plays, notably: *The Seagull* (Orange Tree); *A Man For All Seasons* (York Theatre Royal).

Paul has also recorded many audio books, including *The French Lieutenant's Woman,* for which he won an Earphones Audio Award, *The Kingsley Amis Trilogy* and several Robert Goddard thrillers.

CREATIVES

Indhu Rubasingham
Director

Indhu is the Artistic Director of the Tricycle Theatre.

As Artistic Director: *Handbagged* (Tricycle/ West End); *Paper Dolls*; *Red Velvet* (Tricycle/ St Ann's Warehouse NYC).

Also for the Tricycle: *Women, Power and Politics, Stones In His Pockets, Detaining Justice, The Great Game: Afghanistan, Fabulation, Starstruck.*

Other selected directing credits include: *Belong, Disconnect, Free Outgoing, Lift Off, Clubland, The Crutch, Sugar Mummies* (Royal Court); *Ruined,* (Almeida); *Yellowman, Anna In The Tropics* (Hampstead); *The Waiting Room* (National Theatre); *The Ramayana* (National Theatre/ Birmingham Rep); *Secret Rapture, The Misanthrope* (Minerva, Chichester); *Romeo And Juliet* (Festival Theatre, Chichester); *Pure Gold* (Soho Theatre); *No Boys Cricket Club, Party Girls* (Theatre Royal Stratford East); *Wuthering Heights* (Birmingham Rep.); *Heartbreak House* (Watford Palace); *Sugar Dollies, Shakuntala* (The Gate); *A River Sutra* (Three Mill Island Studios); *Rhinoceros* (UC Davies, California) and *A Doll's House* (Young Vic).

Tom Piper
Designer

Tom is a Creative Associate of the Tricycle Theatre.

For the Tricycle Theatre: *Red Velvet* (Tricycle, NYC), *Bracken Moor.*

Other recent designs include: *Zorro* (Atlanta); Costume designs for *Pride & Prejudice, A Winter's Tale* (Regents Park Open Air Theatre); *Goodbye To All That, Vera Vera Vera* (Royal Court/ Theatre Local); *King Lear* (Citizens' Theatre, Glasgow); *Richard II, The Tempest, As You Like It* (BAM/ Old Vic); *Zorro* (West End/ World Tour); *Dealer's Choice* (Menier Chocolate Factory/ West End); *Falstaff* (Scottish Opera); *Fall* (RSC at the Traverse); *Spyski* (Lyric Hammersmith/ UK tour); *The Scarecrow and His Servant* (Southwark Playhouse); *The Plough and the Stars, The Crucible, Six Characters in Search of an Author* (Abbey Theatre, Dublin).

Tom is the Associate Designer of the RSC. His recent work there includes *Antony and Cleopatra, Boris Godunov, Much Ado About Nothing, Macbeth, City Madam, the Histories Cycle* – for which he won the 2009 Olivier Award for Best Costume Design and was nominated for the 2009 Olivier Award for Best Set Design – *As You Like It, The Grain Store, The Drunks, Antony* and *Cleopatra.*

Elsewhere Tom has worked at the National Theatre, the Donmar, the Royal Opera House, Soho Theatre, Dundee Rep, the Bush, Gate Dublin, Nottingham Playhouse, the Royal Court, Hampstead, Sheffield and in the West End

www.tompiperdesign.co.uk.

Paul Anderson
Lighting Designer

Paul Anderson trained at Mountview Theatre School and York College of Arts and Technology.

Theatre Includes: *A Small Family Business, A Taste of Honey, Amen Corner, This House, Blood and Gifts, Nation, The Revengers Tragedy, A Minute Too Late, Stuff Happens, A Funny Thing Happened on the Way to the Forum, Measure for Measure, Cyrano de Bergerac, The Birds* (National Theatre); *Candide, Two into One, Proof, Torch Song Trilogy, Terrible Advice, Educating Rita, Shirley Valentine, Talent, Little Shop of Horrors* (Menier Chocolate Factory); *A Day in the Death of Joe Egg* (Rose Theatre); *The Mouse and His Child* (RSC); *A Rat's Tale* (Royal Exchange Manchester); *Of Mice and Men* (Watermill Theatre); *The Master and Margarita,* (Complicite - Olivier Award Nomination); *A Dog's Heart* (Complicite/ DNO/ENO co production); *All New People, Educating Rita, Shirley Valentine, Endgame, Arcadia, Treasure Island, Swimming with Sharks, Little Shop of Horrors, Underneath the Lintel, The Tempest, Bent, On The Third Day, Someone Who'll Watch Over Me, A Servant to Two Masters* (West End); *All My Sons* (Broadway); *The Elephant Vanishes, Light, The Noise of Time, Mnemonic* (Drama Desk and Lucille Lortell award); *The Chairs* (Complicite - nominated for Tony, Drama Desk and Olivier awards); *Simply Heavenly* (Young Vic and West End);

The Resistible Rise of Arturo Ui (National Actors Theatre New York, with Al Pacino); *Lenny Henry's So Much Things to Say* (West End and international tour); *Julius Caesar, The Tempest, A Servant to Two Masters* (RSC); *Twelfth Night* (400th anniversary production for Shakespeare's Globe at Middle Temple Hall), *Singer, Americans, The Inland Sea* (Oxford Stage Company); *Two Cities, Playing for Time, Taming of the Shrew* (Salisbury Playhouse); *20,000 Leagues Under the Sea, Shoot to Win, Pinnochio, Sleeping Beauty, Red Riding Hood, Aladdin and Cinderella* (Theatre Royal Stratford East); *The Enchanted Pig, Knight of the Burning Pestle, Simply Heavenly, Arabian Nights, As I lay Dying, Twelfth Night, Guys and Dolls* and *West Side Story* (Young Vic); *Some Girls are Bigger Than Others, Pinocchio, The Threesome,* and *Lyric Nights* (Lyric, Hammersmith); *On Tour, Random and Incomplete Acts of Kindness* (Royal Court); *Turn of the Screw* (Bristol Old Vic).

Opera includes: *Peter Grimes, La Traviata* (Grange Park Opera); *The Rape of Lucricia* (Glyndebourne); *Don Giovanni* (ENO); *Shun-kin, A Disappearing Number, Strange Poetry* (with the LA Philharmonic).

Exhibition credits: *The Christie Brown Exhibition* (Fragments of Narrative at the Wapping Hydraulic Power Station) and *Rediscovering Pompeii at the Academia Italiana* (IBM Exhibition).

Fashion credits: *Fashion East, Lancôme, ghd, Basso & Brooke,* and *AI international.*

Carolyn Downing
Sound Designer

For the Tricycle: *Handbagged* (Tricycle/ West End).

Theatre credits include: *Twelfth Night* (Sheffield Crucible); *Therese Raquin* (Theatre Royal Bath); *Fathers And Sons, Lower Ninth, Dimetos, Absurdia* (Donmar Warehouse); *The Pass, Circle Mirror Transformation, The Low Road, Choir Boy, The Witness, Our Private Life* (Royal Court); *Protest Song, Double Feature* (National Theatre); *The Believers, Beautiful Burnout, Love Song* and *Little Dogs* (Frantic Assembly); *King John, The Gods Weep, The Winter's Tale, Pericles and Days of Significance* (RSC); *Angels in America* (Headlong); *Blackta, After*

Miss Julie (Young Vic); *Much Ado About Nothing, To Kill a Mockingbird, The Country Wife* (Royal Exchange, Manchester); *Blood Wedding* (Almeida); *Lulu, The Kreutzer Sonata, Vanya* (Gate Theatre); *The Water Engine* (Theatre503); *Stallerhof* (Southwark Playhouse); *All My Sons* (Broadway); *Fanny och Alexander* (Malmö Stadsteater); *Amerika, Krieg der Bilder* (Staatstheater, Mainz); *Tre Kronor -Gustav III* (Dramaten, Stockholm).

Opera credits: *How The Whale Became* (ROH); *American Lulu* (The Opera Group); *After Dido* (ENO).

Exhibition credits: *Collider* (Science Museum); *From Street To Trench* (IWM North).

Carolyn was recently awarded the Olivier for Best Sound Design 2014 for her work on *Chimerica* (Almeida/ West End).

Paul Englishby
Composer

For the Tricycle: *Red Velvet* (Tricycle/St Ann's Warehouse, NYC); *Fabulation.*

Theatre includes: *Skylight, The Audience* (West End); *Richard II, Henry IV parts 1&2* among others (RSC – Associate Artist); *A Taste of Honey, Emil and the Detectives* (National Theatre); *Hedda Gabler* (Old Vic); *Children's Children , Marianne Dreams* (Almeida); *South Downs/ The Browning Version* (Chichester/ West End); *The Importance of Being Earnest, Travesties, Wuthering Heights* (Birmingham Rep.); *The Giant, Anna in the Tropics, Yellow Man* (Hampstead); *No Quarter, Sugar Mummies, Blood* (Royal Court); *The Game of Love and Chance, Private Lives,* (Salisbury Playhouse); *Longitude* (Greenwich); *Three Sisters, Romeo and Juliet* (Chichester).

Opera Includes: *The Thief of Baghdad, Pleasure's Progress* (Royal Opera House), *Who is this that comes?* (Opera North).

Television includes: *The Musketeers* (Series 2), *Undeniable, Luther, The Guilty, A Mother's Son, Inside Men, Good Cop, Outcasts, Hamlet, An Englishman in New York, The Score, History of Football, Human Jungle, Pictures on the Piano, Hidden Voices, Living with the Enemy.*

As Arranger: *Dancing on the Edge.*

Film includes: *Girls' Night Out, Salting the Battlefield, Turks and Caicos, Sunshine on Leith, Page Eight, An Education, Miss Pettigrew Lives for a Day, Confetti, Magicians, Ten Minutes Older, The Enlightenment.*

Paul has won an Emmy and two ASCAP awards, and been nominated for the Ivor Novello and BAFTA awards.

Lucy Hind
Movement Director

Lucy trained in choreography, mime and physical theatre at Rhodes University, South Africa and went on to perform with the celebrated First Physical Theatre Company. She is Associate Director of the award winning Slung Low theatre company and a selector for the National Student Drama Festival.

As Movement Director: *Twelfth Night, The Sheffield Mysteries, This Is My Family, Love Your Soldiers* (Sheffield Theatres); *The Jacobin* (Buxton Arts Festival); *Enjoy, Refugee Boy, The Wind in the Willows* (West Yorkshire Playhouse); *Manchester Sound: The Massacre* (Library Theatre); *Stuart: A Life Backwards* (Hightide/ Edinburgh).

As Co-Director: *Extra-Ordinary* (UK Tour).

As a Dancer: *The Impending Storm* (DanceXchange/ Unlimited Festival/ Southbank Centre); *Boundless* (Dance Xchange).

As Dance Captain: London 2012 Paralympics Opening Ceremony (LOCOG);

Television includes: *Peter Pan* (BBC); *Banana* (E4/ Red Productions).

Harry Mackrill
Assistant Director

Harry is Resident Director at the Tricycle Theatre.

For the Tricycle: *The Colby Sisters of Pittsburgh, Pennsylvania; Handbagged* (Associate, West End); *Red Velvet* (Tricycle/ St Ann's Warehouse, NYC).

Directing credits include: *This Isn't a Thing, Right?* (Nabokov Arts Club); *Coffee & Whisky* (Ovalhouse); *Look Back in Anger* (New Wimbledon Studio).

Assistant Directing includes: *Casualties* (Park Theatre); *Mother Courage* (Library Theatre, Manchester); *I Gaze From My Kitchen Like An Astronaut* (Jaybird Live Literature).

Briony Barnett
Casting Director

For the Tricycle Theatre: *The Colby Sisters of Pittsburgh, Pennsylvania; Handbagged* (Tricycle/ West End) and *One Monkey Don't Stop No Show.*

Theatre includes: *The Royal Duchess Superstore* (The Broadway, Half Moon); *Fences* (Theatre Royal Bath, West End).

Film includes: *What We Did On Our Holiday, Travellers, The Borderlands, High Tide, Stop, Janet and Bernard, Common People, The Knot, 10 by 10.*

Television includes: *Outnumbered, Inside the Mind of Leonardo.*

Darren Lang
Magic Consultant

For Tricycle Theatre: *The Arabian Nights.*

Theatre Includes: *Annie Get Your Gun* (UK); *Witches of Eastwick* (Watermill Theatre); *Afraid Of The Dark* (Charing Cross Theatre); *Brilliant Adventures, Dr Faustus* (Royal Exchange, Manchester); *Peter Pan* (Octagon Theatre, Bolton); *Alice in Wonderland* (New Vic Theatre); *Some Like It Hip Hop* (Peacock Theatre); *A Midsummer Night's Dream* (Almeida/ Edinburgh); *Doctor Faustus* (Creation Theatre Co.); *Newsrevue* (Pleasance, Edinburgh); *Darker Shores* (Hampstead).

Opera includes: *The Queen Of Spades* (Grange Park Opera); *Il Ritorno D'ulisse In Patria* (Royal Northern College of Music).

Associate work includes: *The Phantom of The Opera* (UK Tour); *Mrs Affleck* (National Theatre); *Aladdin* (Hackney Empire).

SUPPORT US

The Tricycle is committed to bringing unheard voices into the mainstream and to presenting the world through different lenses — we are a place where cultures connect and creativity flourishes.

We need to raise £3 million over the next three years to realise our ambitions to produce theatre that questions and entertains, support our work with young people in the local community, and transform the Tricycle in a £7 million capital project.

The support we receive from grant-making charitable trusts, corporate partners and individual donors is more important than ever; please join us at this important time in the Tricycle's history.

With your support, we can continue to:

- create world-class theatre, like our Olivier award-winning production Handbagged and the critically acclaimed *Red Velvet*;

- deliver over 22,000 Creative Learning experiences annually for young people in Brent and beyond to inspire a diverse new generation of theatre-makers and audiences;

- transform the Tricycle into a welcoming space, with a more flexible, accessible and sustainable building in which to see and make theatre.

Thank you in advance for your support

JOIN US TODAY

Our members receive a wide range of benefits across stage and screen, with priority booking on tickets, invitations to member events, discounted theatre tickets, and opportunities to observe our Creative Learning work.

Membership starts from just £125 per year.

To join or for further details, please visit www.tricycle.co.uk/support, or telephone the Development Department on 020 7625 0132.

THANK YOU

We are extremely grateful to our supporters, whose help has made the work we produce at the Tricycle Theatre possible year after year. Thank you for your support.

PUBLIC FUNDING

TRUSTS AND FOUNDATIONS

 AN ROINN GNÓTHAÍ EACHTRACHA AGUS TRÁDÁLA NA hÉIREANN
DEPARTMENT OF FOREIGN AFFAIRS AND TRADE OF IRELAND

MediaTrust

STANLEY THOMAS JOHNSON FOUNDATION

Anya Evans Jones Foundation

BBC Children in Need

The Bertha Foundation

95.8 Capital FM's Help a Capital Child

The Coutts Charitable Trust

Dischma Charitable Trust

The A. M. Dommett Charitable Trust

D'Oyly Carte Charitable Trust

John Ellerman Foundation

Esmée Fairbairn Foundation

Equity Charitable Trust

Garfield Weston Foundation

Robert Gavron Charitable Trust

J Paul Getty Jnr Charitable Trust

The Helen Hamlyn Trust

Irish Youth Foundation

London Schools Excellence Fund

John Lyon's Charity

The Mactaggart Third Fund

Marie-Louise von Motesiczky Charitable Trust

Network Stadium Housing Association

A New Direction

The Prince's Foundation for Children and the Arts

Sir Siegmund Warburg's Voluntary Settlement

The Stanley Foundation

The Topinambour Trust

Vanderbilt Family Foundation

Vandervell Foundation

Harold Hyam Wingate Foundation

INDIVIDUALS

Major Donors
Jon & NoraLee Sedmak
Robert Brass

Director's Circle
Liz Astaire
Christopher Bevan
Chris Hogg
Jeremy Lewison & Caroline
  Schuck

Pioneer
Jennie Bland
Kay Ellen Consolver & John
  Storkerson
Gillian Frumkin
Judy Lever
Andree Molyneux
John Reiss
Marjorie & Albert Scardino
Carol Sellars
Joseph and Sarah Zarfaty

Front Wheel
David & Jenny Altschuler
Primrose & David Bell
Helen & Keith Bolderson
Katie Bradford
Fiona Calnan
Lady Hatch
Michael Farthing & Alison
  McLean
Anya & Grant Jones

Innovator
Nadhim Ahmed
Sue Allett
Henry Chu & James Baer
Noreen Doyle
Claire Godwin
Tony & Melanie Henderson
Harold & Valerie Joels
Lady Diane Lever
Colette & Peter Levy
John & Margaret Mann
Posgate Charitable Trust
Sir Peter Roth
Jackie Rothenberg
Rajeev Samaranayake
Professor Audrey Sheiham

Supporter
Martin Blackburn
Mrs L Colchester
Lily and Anthony Filer
Rosita & Brian Green
Barbara Hosking
Christine Jackson
Isabelle Laurent
Dr & Mrs Papadakis
Pauline Swindells
Joan Weil

Cinema Box
Steven & Sharon Baruch
David Cohen
Veronica Cohen
Gerry & Kim Davis
Jack Gold
Fiona Finlay
Roda Fisher & Michael
  Hannaway

Bird & Alan Hovell
Anna Jansz
Ann & Gerard Kieran
Christopher Kitching
Jenifer Landor
Monique Law
John & Rose Lebor
Isabel Martorell
M P Moran & Sons Ltd
Isabel Morgan
Terry Munyard
Gina Newson
Catherine Roe
John & Melanie Roseveare
Philip Saville
Glenis Scadding
Isabelle & Ivor Seddon
Barrie Tankel
Eliana Tomkins
Maggie Turp
Sandar Warshal and Family
Christine & Tom Whiteside

**The Tricycle would also like
to thank our Trailblazers,
Friends and all anonymous
donors.**

Corporate Partners
The Clancy Group PLC
Casareccia
Daniel & Harris Solicitors
J. Leon & Company Ltd
JPC Law
London Walks Ltd
Mulberry House School
The North London Tavern

CREATIVE LEARNING

Young People
The Tricycle has always been known for its work providing inspirational opportunities that improve the lives of young people. Whether as audiences, writers, performers or producers of new

Our Projects
Our work in the local community reaches out to marginalised young people. We work in mainstream and special needs education, with young asylum seekers and refugees and with children in some of Brent's – and the UK's - most deprived areas. The Tricycle helps give all these people a voice, and the confidence to articulate it.

Tricycle Young Company offers 11–25 year olds the chance to make high quality theatre productions; developing skills, confidence and professionalism through work with the highest calibre artists. Our first ever Takeover Festival took place during one week in April 2014, when over 200 young people programmed concerts, masterclasses and film screenings and presented 10 new theatre productions.

If you want to know about Creative Learning at the Tricycle, please contact us on creativelearning@tricycle.co.uk or 020 7625 0134.

New for 2014: Story Lab
Plays for children, invented by children

This autumn we are inviting 300 Brent primary school pupils to visit the Tricycle Story Lab. Children will be working with our special 'Story Scientists' who will adapt their brilliant ideas for our stage and improve their reading, writing and inventing skills.

Department
for Education

SUPPORTED BY
MAYOR OF LONDON

FOR THE TRICYCLE

Introduction

Marcus Gardley's lyrical play, *The House That Will Not Stand*, is haunted by so much more than the ghost that promises to destroy the titular house. In many ways the play's patriarchal ghost, Lazare Albans, is a MacGuffin, a misleading plot device that remains enigmatic. Audiences will hear ghostly echoes of other canonical plays that include patriarchal apparitions. In *The House That Will Not Stand*, the ghost of the father demands, but his story, will, and cultural legacy are already destined to be forgotten. The women's history is the one that must be unearthed and experienced, and Gardley asks not only what it means to be a part of a culture that practices historical amnesia but also what it takes to remember. What happens when we remember something that has been so deeply buried by our society? What do we do with the cultural-historical remains we excavate?

Marcus Gardley is part of the cohort of young, black American playwrights who have been labeled by Harry Elam, Jr. as the "new post-black practitioners": artists who came to artistic distinction in the "Age of Obama."[1] Included in this group are slightly more established playwrights like Suzan-Lori Parks and Lynn Nottage, and younger playwrights like Eisa Davis, Katori Hall, Branden Jacob-Jenkins, and Tarell Alvin McCraney. As Harry Elam, Jr. explains, inclusion in the cohort is usually defined by the fact that post-black playwrights search to find "new and multiple expressions of blackness unburdened by the social and cultural expectations of the past."[2] While this may seem to be at odds with Gardley's historical approach, *The House That Will Not Stand* asks its audience to interrogate how racial constructions shift, change and radically metamorphose over time. Race is not a stable category despite the dominant narrative that gets consistently recycled in American culture,

1. Harry Elam, Jr., "Post-World War II African American Theatre," in *Oxford Handbook of American Drama*, ed. Jeffrey Richards and Heather S. Nathans (Oxford: Oxford University Press, 2014), p. 389.

2. Ibid.

and Gardley's play effectively denaturalizes the notion of race's singular construct: it reveals and enables multiple expressions of blackness.

Set in New Orleans in 1836, *The House That Will Not Stand* takes place in the liminal moment after the Louisiana Purchase in 1803 and before the outbreak of the Civil War in 1860. Louisiana became a French colony in the early eighteenth century, but was ceded to the Spanish in 1762 in order to lure Spain to fight against the British in the French and Indian War. To the chagrin of the still-nascent United States, the First Consul of the Republic of France, Napoleon Bonaparte, acquired Louisiana from Spain on October 1, 1800. While the US government successfully completed the Louisiana Purchase in 1803 (with statehood ratified in 1812), the culture of Louisiana remained unique and distinct from the rest of the American states and territories.

Unlike most American colonies, the Louisiana territory under both the French and Spanish developed a mixed-race class that included numerous free people of color (*gens de couleur libres*). Because the territory was not initially envisioned as a settler colony, there were few European women who lived in Louisiana in the eighteenth century. Thus, it became a common practice for the male European colonists to take enslaved African women as mistresses or even as common-law wives, and their children were distinguished racially as being colored (instead of black) and were frequently freed from slavery. As a result, a unique class of free people of color and the system of *plaçage* emerged – an extra-legal financial system in which mixed-race mistresses and common-law wives, and their mixed-race offspring, could negotiate for and be willed freedom, property, money, and education. In effect, the Louisiana territory under French and Spanish rule created a three-tiered racial system (like those in Brazil, Cuba, and Haiti) that disaggregated persons of African descent not only by their status as free or enslaved, but also by their color (darker or lighter than a brown paper bag) and wealth. When Louisiana became an American territory and then a state, *plaçage* survived as a custom for a while but it was increasingly challenged on legal grounds. In effect, the Americanization of Louisiana meant that a binaristic view of race (black/white) became codified.

Marcus Gardley has said that he sat down to write a play about his own experiences growing up in late-twentieth-century Oakland, California, but found himself disinterring a story about nineteenth-century New Orleans, Louisiana. For Gardley, the explicit connection between these locations and histories was his family's migration from NOLA to Oaktown. The implicit connection is Gardley's interest in the way certain stories become the stuff of official history while others get buried, lost, forgotten and written over. Gardley saw glimpses of the palimpsest in his own family's history and set out to uncover the underlying narratives of color, money, power and freedom. Taken as a whole, *The House That Will Not Stand* beautifully confronts current narratives about race and freedom.

On the most basic level, Gardley reveals the complex color distinctions that were used to divide blacks and define beauty. Although Beartrice Albans, the free woman of color who is Lazare Albans' *placée*, has three free-born daughters, they are distinguished by their color. The oldest Agnès "is the color of butter," the middle Maude Lynn "is white as milk," and the youngest Odette "is brown as oatmeal." While it is clear that "their beauty is astonishing," the characters see important defining differences in their hues. Far from depicting these color distinctions as essential, though, *The House That Will Not Stand* shows how societies must inculcate individuals about the differences. Agnès tells her youngest and darkest sister that part of growing up is realizing that black is not beautiful.

> No one's told you the truth 'cause they didn't want to hurt you but since we're going out into the grown-up world, I figure it's time you became a woman. You're dark, Odette. You've got more brown than the paper bag. This means you wear the stain in our blood that we so desperately try to hide . . . And that means you have no choice in life – you're at the bottom.

Odette has always had a positive view of herself because she
was not aware of the significance of the paper bag principle –
that beauty is restricted to skin tones lighter than a brown bag.
In nineteenth-century New Orleans, though, growing into
womanhood is defined by one's ability to internalize social
constructions for race and beauty. Nonetheless, the revelation
that the constructs must be *taught* by definition renders them
unnatural. Seen from our twenty-first-century vantage point,
the current binary structure for race in the United States is
completely deconstructed by *The House That Will Not Stand*: it
is one of the many houses that is revealed to have been built
on a sinkhole.

The House That Will Not Stand also asks the audience to reconsider
African-American spiritual life. The play is infused with music,
chants and incantations that empower the women to imagine
alternative social and historical realities. While Maude Lynn is
depicted as an impassioned Christian, she is also the character
who is the most, well, maudlin (as her name suggests). In
contrast, the slave Makeda, who sings "Hey Papa Legba," the
Vodou song that opens the gates to the spiritual world, is filled
with a life that cannot be contained by the play (she exits singing).
After all, she is the one who remembers and reanimates their
African heritage, identifying the drum as the externalized form
their souls embody. She chants to the drum, calling out to
remember a past that is available to "Us. We. Kin of Kulekini,
cousins of Nkumu":

> Wake up! See how we survived
> Come quick kin!
> Come from every seed and bloodline
> Come, you who have only one drop
> You who have passed for such a long time
> Come, you white as the Lamb
> Brown as the furrowed brow
> Yellow as teeth
> Black as the shadow of an eye
> Come you who didn't know you was livin a lie.

Like the famous Harlem Renaissance poem by Countee Cullen, "Heritage," Marcus Gardley invites his audience to ask, "What is Africa to me?" For Makeda, it is a heritage that unites and empowers all regardless of hue, but her last words suggest that one's heritage can only take one so far: "Only I can get me across / I got one more river to cross / Just one more river to cross." While the African-American Christian spiritual is frequently figured as the key to strength, forgiveness and uplift, Gardley's play places Christian spirituality in a continuum with African and Haitian practices.

Likewise, *The House That Will Not Stand* denaturalizes contemporary assumptions about freedom. While the Albans women are all free-born, they define freedom in radically different ways. The matriarch Beartrice defines freedom as complete financial independence. When Lazare's ghost complains that she "had it easy," she retorts that she only received material gains as long as she "opened [her] legs and kept [her] mouth shut." Thus, she assumes her daughters will not want to be *placées* if she obtains financial independence in the form of the deed to their home. Of course, this turns out not to be the case, because all the women in the play define freedom differently. For instance, Beartrice's clairvoyant sister Marie Josephine defines freedom as the opportunity to marry a *black man*, one who plays the *bamboulas* in Congo Square. For Marie Josephine being free only comes with the freedom to choose one's partner regardless of color or race. And the youngest and darkest Albans, beautiful Odette, defines freedom as an ability to see herself for herself – not as others see her, but as she sees herself in her own skin. While Toni Morrison's famous novel *Beloved* asks its reader to imagine how a lack of legal freedom can drive a good mother to murder her child, Marcus Gardley asks us to imagine if, how, and when freedom is defined beyond the simplistic binary of enslaved and legally free.

I realize this introduction makes *The House That Will Not Stand* sound dreadfully serious because the play's contexts, themes, and literary allusions are weighty, but the play has a remarkable levity. Part of the play's lyricism comes from its humor, playfulness and lively spirit; its tone and tenor are beautifully buoyant. The house depicted in Gardley's play will collapse, but his invitation to work through what it means to remember it will, I hope, live beyond his two-hours' traffic on the stage.

Ayanna Thompson
George Washington University, 2014

The House That Will Not Stand

A drama about the free women of color
in New Orleans, 1836

Good taste was out of place in the company of
death, death itself was the essence of bad taste. And
there must be much rage and saliva in its presence.
The body must move and throw itself about, the eyes
must roll, the hands should have no peace, and the
throat should release all the yearning, despair and
outrage that accompany the stupidity of loss.

Toni Morrison, *Sula*

A house divided against itself cannot stand.

Mark 3:25

He who cannot dance will say the drum is bad.

African proverb

Characters

Lazare Albans, *seventy-two, a wealthy white merchant*
Beartrice Albans, *fifty, a free woman of color, his mistress*
Agnès Albans, *nineteen, their eldest daughter, sensual (pronounced 'An-yes')*
Maude Lynn Albans, *eighteen, the middle daughter − the lightest, spiritual*
Odette Albans, *sixteen, the youngest daughter − the darker, romantic*
Makeda, *forty, a house servant, black and regal*
La Veuve, *forty-five, a free woman of color, Beartrice's sworn enemy*
Marie Josephine, *forty, Beartrice's sister; a clairvoyant*

Setting

Faubourg Tremé, New Orleans, Louisiana, twenty-four hours one summer Sunday in 1836.

Notes

The dialogue moves at a rapid pace. Words in italics are Louisiana French Creole. Words indented are sung. Words in italics are stressed. All sound and music should come from live actors to emphasize the natural world.

A (/) indicates overlapping dialogue.

Please note: these women are grand but not melodramatic, proud but not impolite. Their comedy seeps from a keen sense of wit and their meanness, though served with grace, cuts into the bone and leaves a scar for life.

Act One

The dead body of **Lazare Albans**, *seventy-two, lies stiff as birdshit on a table in the parlor room of a Creole cottage. Surrounded by gardenias and stuffed in a pearly white suit, he looks so pretty one could weep over him or float him in a parade. Yet his beauty is no match for the walls, which are white as God's teeth and the wooden floor, which sparkles like brand-new patent-leather shoes. Three life-size paintings of exceedingly beautiful colored women (poised like queens) hang between four French windows covered in black crêpe. A red, velvet chaise sits in the right corner downstage, beside an orchid and a throne-like chair etched in African symbols. This is the tearoom. A chandelier made of pearls and cowry shells hangs over the room and gives the only glimmer of light (candlelight) since the windows and mirrors are covered. Even the clocks have been stopped. This is a house shrouded in the lifeless music of mourning.*

Enter **La Veuve**, *forty-five, a tall, elegant free woman of color. She is prepared to give the performance of her life. She wails (dry-eyed) all the way up to* **Lazare**'s *casket, hiding her visage behind a black fan until she realizes she is alone. She notices rings on the dead man's fingers and steals them.*

There is only one that she cannot pry free. She puts her back into it and pulls! She supposedly gets 'touched' by the corpse.

La Veuve   Sweet Jesus Almighty!

Makeda   You called?

Enter **Makeda**, *forty, with tea. She is dark, beautiful as the day is long. Her hair is wrapped in an orange-gold-red tignon.*

La Veuve   I've been violated.

Makeda   Already? You just got here.

La Veuve   He touched me!

Makeda   By 'he' you mean?

La Veuve   He! Him! There! Lazare!

Makeda   You sho, *ma'amzelle*, 'cause he's dead.

La Veuve   I know that, I know he dead! Why you think I come here dressed in my best black? Walked all the way from Jackson Square just to pray and pay my respects and he's gonna manhandle me. I know when I've been touched *and I've been touched.*

Makeda   Touched in the head.

La Veuve   *Excuse-moi?*

Makeda   Man probably couldn't help himself, he likes to touch meat. When he was alive, if he didn't have his hands on a chicken leg he had it on my thigh. I used to have to put honey on my breasts just so he'd get sticky fingers and stop. Now if he was that touchy-feely in life, it make sense he'd be somewhat so in death. He probably on his way to hell and needed to cop one last feel before the fire.

La Veuve   It's the devil's work when dead bodies move without permission, Makeda. His spirit must be unsettled. He probably died bad and his ghost is tryin to haunt this house. He probably touched me because he was tryin to tell me something.

Makeda   Maybe he was tryin to tell you to keep your fingers off his rings.

La Veuve   Rings? You must be seeing things. What rings?

Makeda   Those rings on your fingers.

La Veuve   Oh, these. Please, I was just tryin them on.

Makeda   Sho you was and tryin my patience.

La Veuve *gives her the rings.*

La Veuve   Well, I guess you know it all then, don't you?

Makeda   I do and you know it.

La Veuve   Did you know Monsieur Lazare is not the first of Beartrice's lovers to die from unnatural causes?

Makeda   Who said the cause was unnatural? The man was seventy-two. He walked like a pigeon, drunk like a fish, and ate like a stray dog. If you ask me, God should have put him down decades ago.

La Veuve   But look at his eyes. If he died natural why are his eyes in a state of fright? When a body goes in peace, the irises of the eyes, they wither into the soft hues of morning. But when a body dies bad, the eyes burn bloodshot like a sunset. They tell the story of someone who's been frightened, struck by fever . . . *or murdered*!

Makeda   Murdered? Lord of Mercy, you giving me the chills. I best pour myself some tea.

She pours tea.

La Veuve   Good, 'cause that's why I'm really here. I need you to pour the tea, Makeda.

Makeda   Good, 'cause that's what I'm doing, *ma'amzelle* –

La Veuve   *Non*, Makeda I need you to *pour the tea*. The tea about how Lazare died.

Makeda   Oh, I can't pour that. That tea is secret.

La Veuve   But I won't tell a soul. I swallow secrets, I don't spill them. I just want to *taste* your tea. I promise not to let a drop fall from my lips, I give you my word. See . . .

She gives **Makeda** *a half-dime.*

La Veuve   It's golden.

Makeda   Would you look at that. My favorite color. I guess I could pour you a sip then. Though if I had something sweeter to put in my pot, I could probably pour you a whole cup.

La Veuve   I see somebody's got a sweet tooth.

Makeda   *Oui ma'amzelle*, all my teeth are sweet.

She smiles.

La Veuve   How about a whole dime? How does that fit your taste?

She gives **Makeda** *another dime.* **Makeda** *bites the coin to taste.*

Makeda   It's tasteful. But it ain't sweeeet, *ma'amzelle*. It ain't that good sugar that brightens your smile and puts a pretty pep in your step. I likes things syrupy sweet. What other treats you got in your bag?

La Veuve   Somebody's got an appetite. How about a quarter piece –

Makeda *snatches the coin.*

Makeda   A quarter will work. Now it's best we drink this tea before the *madame* gets back from church.

She pours tea, leaning in to gossip.

Maître Lazare died thirteen hours ago. Be why I stopped all the clocks on the exact stroke of his death – six beats pass midnight. Then I covered the mirrors and cleaned his body for wake. *Madame* Beartrice insisted upon it, detailing each task like she had been planning it for weeks. She told her daughters that the house was to go into mourning for seven months in honor of their father, the only white man she loved as much as Jesus. Now if that don't make you scratch your head, don't chew your nails, it gets itchier in a minute. She had his shoes and suit picked out by eight. By nine, she had the embalmer gut his guts and by ten she had paid a long visit to his estranged wife. By eleven, she had six dozen gardenias brought to beautify his body and a *coiffure* to do her and her daughters' hair. By twelve, she was dressed in full mourning: a *calotte*, long black veil and enough tears in her eyes to baptize the whole congregation at St. Augustine's, which is where she is now, playing the grieving widow with the acting chops of a two-faced politician. But here's the real itch: thirteen hours ago, before *Maître* Lazare died, he and the *madame* were at each other's throat. I saw it unfold from my peephole in the kitch where I was sippin chickory. The *maître* came home carrying three new gowns for his daughters to wear to the masked ball, only to find out that the *madame* was not letting them go for the fifth year in a row. She told him that she would rather die than see her daughters become *placeés* and thusly the property of white men even if it meant increasing the family fortune. Well, this made the *maître* so heated, he leapt in the air like a loose firecracker, cracklin curses and swinging his fist so wild you thought he was having a fit and needed to be tied. *Madame* did her best to dance around his swings but both of them ended up on the floor, wrestling like Jacob and the angel. It was such a sight I couldn't watch 'em with both eyes.

She keeps her right eye open.

So I kept my good eye on them for as long as I could. That's when the *maître* got hold of the *madame,* lifted her high in the air and squeezed her throat so tight the poor woman could barely catch her breath . . .

Makeda *loses her breath.*

La Veuve   Then what? What happened then?

Makeda   Funny thing is, I can't quite remember. My memory's gotten so bad as of late, I must be getting old. Maybe if you run some coins pass me, it'll help jog my remembrance.

La Veuve   I don't have any more coins, you cleaned out my bag.

Makeda   But I didn't slap your wrist. You got the prettiest bracelets round them wrists –

La Veuve   I can't part with these, they're priceless.

Makeda   Come now, everything got a price. You talking to a slave.

La Veuve   Fine then, take 'em but you got to hurry.

*She gives **Makeda** her bracelets.*

Makeda   Not to worry, every story can be cut to the chase. Just let me try these bangles on for size, make sure they . . . Dear God, would you look at this. These chains be golden on me. I wonder if they come with matching earrings.

La Veuve *hands her the earrings.*

La Veuve   You're trying my patience now, gal. Speak! What happened when Beartrice couldn't catch her breath?

Makeda   She turned blue of course. With the *maître*'s hand clenched around her throat I thought she'd surely die. But suddenly the poor man caught a chill, started trembling and then he dropped to the floor like a block of ice. That's when I heard a scream. So I ran. Ran fast as feet could carry and when I arrived in the sitting room, the *madame* was bleeding from the lip and limpin by the foot but the *maître* was still, lying cold, hand over his heart and dead as horse without a head.

La Veuve   I knew it! She killed him.

Makeda   Didn't say that. Didn't say she killed him. Besides Dr. Phillipe said he died of a heart attack.

La Veuve   What Dr. Phillipe know? The man said I was coldblooded so you know he can't be no real doctor. Beartrice killed him. She probably whispered a voo doo blues in his ear and froze his heart into a sickle.

Makeda   Awl, here you go. Folks is always blaming voo doo for 'who do' they don't understand. The *Madame* don't even know no voo doo.

La Veuve   But you do, don't you, Makeda? Did you give her the spell?

Makeda   Who says I know how to spell? Who says I even know how to read? I'm a slave.

La Veuve   Some say certain slaves can master words better than those that are free. Some say you learned your ways from that conjure woman Marie LaVeau. They say you and her are as close as lips.

Makeda   Sounds like you heard a lot of hearsay. If I were you, I wouldn't house everything I hear. I didn't give the *madame* no spell and I don't let folks play in my black bag. Besides, the *madame* is not a killer. She may be crass, calculating and unkind but a killer she is not.

La Veuve   She's got your head in the clouds, Makeda. Open your eyes. The winds have changed; the tide has turned. Napoleon has sold Louisiana to those slew-footed, land-thieving *Americains* and by this time tomorrow, New Orleans will be kneelin at the feet of Yankees. Free people of color will lose their rights, slaves will lose any chance of buying their freedom and any woman without property will be looked upon as a harlot. You must act now. You must get free soon or you will be her servant for the rest of your miserable life. You and I both know Beartrice has no intention of signing your papers. You've been her property for over twenty years and she won't even let you have half a holiday. But if she's in prison . . . if you tell the authorities she killed Lazare, all of her assets will be sold to the highest bidder, you will be up for auction and that's when I'll buy you and set you free as the birds.

Makeda   Why come? Why would you do that for me?

La Veuve   Oh, I don't know, perhaps it's because I'm sweet. Or perhaps it's because it's my greatest wish in this small stretch of life to snatch Beartrice Albans down from her high horse, take this house from her tight embrace and watch her die penniless and pathetic in some prison like the rat she is. Her: sticking her nose up at me, telling folks I don't have Creole blood, taking my lovers, spreading gossip and weaving lies. But soon, sweet Jesus I get to cut her like cane! (*Soft.*) Won't you help me, Makeda?

Makeda   I don't know, this all seems sudden. What about her daughters? I raised those gals – if the *madame* is put in jail, they'll have to fend for themselves. They've been sheltered all of their lives, they'll be preyed upon, kidnapped, eaten or starved –

La Veuve   *Oui*, probably. But you'll be free. Today is a new day, Makeda. Gird your loins! It's every woman for her own self.

Outside, three sisters enter counting rosaries. Their beauty is astonishing. The eldest, **Agnès** *(pronounced An-yes), is the color of butter, the middle child,* **Maude Lynn**, *is white as milk and the youngest,* **Odette**, *is brown as oatmeal. They stop once they reach the porch.*

Agnès, **Maude Lynn** *and* **Odette**

(mournfully singing)	*(translation)*
Salve Regina,	*Hail, O Queen,*
Mater misericordiae	*Mother of mercy*
Vita dulcedo,	*Our life, our sweetness,*
Et spes nostra salve.	*And our hope, hail.*
Ad te clamamus,	*To thee do we cry,*
Exsules filia Hevae	*Exiles; daughters of Eve*
Ad te suspiramus,	*To thee do we sigh*
Gementes et flentes	*Moaning and weeping*
In hac lacrimarum valle.	*In this valley of tears.*

Overwhelmed with grief, **Maude Lynn** *falls to her knees, sobbing.*

Odette   *Pauvre*, Maude Lynn. She's so full of sorrow, her legs can't carry her and her heavy heart. Grab her other shoulder, Agnès. We're sisters, let's help her to her feet.

Agnès *walks on the other side to help her.*

Odette   If we can't lean on each other then we're all doomed to fall.

Agnès   Come now, Maude Lynn, you must try and stand. *Maman* say a good woman must stand for something sometime in her life –

Maude Lynn   He's dead. *Mon père* is dead and he's never coming back.

Agnès   *Bien sur*, that's what dead means: it means you're never comin –

Odette   Agnès, try and show some sympathy: sympathize.
He was our father.

Agnès   *Alors*, Maude Lynn, look at the bright side, at least
you'll get to see him again when you die –

Odette   Agnès!

Agnès   I mean, in *Heaven*, and oh, what a glorious day that
will be.

Maude Lynn   But it won't. *Mon père* is not going to heaven.

Agnès   He's not?

Maude Lynn   Of course not! Don't you read the Bible?

Agnès   Not religiously but I've skimmed a few pages. There's
just so many words –

Maude Lynn   The word of the Lord says *mon père* is going
straight to hell for being an adulterer, a cheat, a curse, a liar,
a drunk, a heretic and a sloth. We were as close as praying
hands. He confided in me but I could not save his soul.

Odette   Come now, *Père* was sinful but he did good deeds on
Earth as well. For one, he never put his hands on us, he bought
us most things we wanted and at night he kissed our eyes into
dream.

Agnès   *Ah la la*, Odette, you're so romantic you're giving me
heartburn. The man's dead. Might as well tell the truth and
shame the devil: *mon père* barely knew us.

Maude Lynn   Agnès!

Agnès   *Oui*, at night he kissed us into dream. But during the
day he kept us at arms' length, treated us like porcelain dolls
with empty heads. He was a man: a good businessman who
knew the value of bodies and blood and good breeding; he
was our patron and in some ways we were his greatest
possession. Therefore the best way to remember him is not to
weep for his soul but to take a page out of his billfold. We must
become *placées*. *Mon père* did his best when he was alive to

convince *Maman* to let us go to the ball and now that he's dead we must pick up the banner. We must find a white man with good blood and good fortune, bed him and take all his money. We must show the world why men come all the way from France to sell their hearts to free colored women. We must do this soon, before the Yankees come with their savage slave laws and rule New Orleans like cattlemen. We're Creoles: we must be vigilant yet gentile. We must have faith. Even God responds to faith. That's why He dropped a miracle in my lap today during Mass. I got a sign: a letter: a love letter.

Odette   A love letter? You mean like from a man?

Maude Lynn   And in church?!

Agnès   *Oui, mais oui* and his name's Ràmon Le Pip.

Odette   O Agnès, that love letter could lead to true love –

Maude Lynn   And straight into a den of sin.

Agnès   I know, but I can't get my hopes up. If I play my cards right, this letter could get me free by sunrise.

She takes the letter from between her breasts as her sisters surround her.

Beartrice   *Attention!!*

Enter **Beartrice**. *She pounds her cane and the sisters fall into single file like soldiers.*

Agnès, **Maude Lynn** *and* **Odette**   *Oui, Maman.*

Beartrice   Should be ashamed. Your father hasn't been dead a whole day and you're standin around cacklin like a bunch of rump-ugly witches. It's a disgrace. *Marchons!*

Agnès, **Maude Lynn** *and* **Odette**   *Oui, Maman. Tout de suite.*

They enter the house, **Beartrice** *in the lead.* **Makeda** *is still talking to* **La Veuve**.

Beartrice   Look at this place!

Makeda   Oops, got to work –

Makeda *cleans, then exits.*

Beartrice   It looks filthy as a whore's mouth in here.

They enter into the tearoom. **Beartrice** *sits on a throne. The others sit on a chaise.*

La Veuve   Afternoon, *Madame Albans*.

Beartrice   *La Veuve.* (*Under her breath.*) Speak of whores and one shows up.

La Veuve   *Koman sa va?*

Beartrice   *Mo bon*, and yourself?

La Veuve   Feeling a bit light as of late but I'm here to pay my respects. You've gotten sickly I see. Pale. Must be grief. How are you holding up?

Beartrice   I'm kicking but not high.

La Veuve   Was wondering what happened to your foot?

Beartrice   Tripped on a stone.

La Veuve   Course. Sooner or later, even the high and mighty fall.

Beartrice   We all fall. It's how a woman lands that makes her a lady. Well, don't just stand there, *mes filles*. Acknowledge our guest!

Agnès, Maude Lynn *and* **Odette**   *Bonjour Madame La Veuve?*

La Veuve   *Bonjour, les anges.*

Beartrice   *La Veuve*, you will forgive the state of *ma maison*. I prefer keeping an immaculate house but since it's the Sabbath most of our servants are taking a day of rest.

La Veuve   Don't be silly, your home is –

She rubs her finger across the furniture.

– clean as can be.

Beartrice   It's clean for some but I know dirt when I see it.

She gives **La Veuve** *a dirty look.*

Beartrice   Will you join us for tea?

La Veuve   With pleasure. It's been a long stretch since someone poured me some tea.

Beartrice   Is that so? MAKEDA! Bring us hot tea and beignets.

Makeda (*offstage*)   We ain't got no more beignets, *madame*!

Beartrice   Then serve praw-leans! We can't have tea without sweets.

Odette   What about iced tea, *Maman*? It's rather hot –

Agnès   I know I'm hot and bothered.

Beartrice   Nonsense. Iced tea is for toothless biddies and overweight infants. We're in mourning: we drink hot tea to soothe our grief and dry our tears.

I see you are without your jewelry, *Madame La Veuve*. That's unlike you. One must be careful these days, I hear even the servants can grease the gold off your bones right before your eyes.

La Veuve   Well, I was in a giving mood this morn and gave my gold to charity.

Beartrice   Oh, Albans would be moved; he had a heart for the poor.

Maude Lynn *weeps.*

Beartrice   Maude Lynn, if you start that incessant weeping, I will make you lie under your bed. We don't cry in front of company – it's self-indulgent. Wait till nightfall if you want to weep a river.

Maude Lynn   *Oui, Maman. Repose en paix, mon père.*

Everyone gives the sign of the cross.

Beartrice   Maude Lynn loved him most, she's something holy. If she was ugly I'd make her be a nun but her face is too pretty for a habit. She's got a good soul though, unlike these two. The youngest, Odette, is all heart and the oldest, Agnès, all body. But they wise like me and tough as teeth.

Maude Lynn *whimpers.*

Beartrice   Stop that sniffling! Sniffling is for opium addicts and infants with pneumonia.

Maude Lynn   *Oui Maman.*

La Veuve   She's just grieving, Beartrice. Be soft.

Beartrice   Oh, I didn't know you had children, *Madame La Veuve?*

La Veuve   I don't and you know it.

Beartrice   Don't I . . .

She snaps open a fan and cools herself. Her daughters follow suit. They all wave their fans to the same rhythm. **Makeda** *enters with tea and pralines.*

Makeda   Tea is served, *madame.*

Beartrice   *Bon.* (*To* **La Veuve.**) What do you know of this new arrival from Marseille, a young man by the name of Ràmon Le Pip?

La Veuve   Not much. Just know he's so rich he buys a new boat anytime the other one gets wet. His father is a fur trader like your Lazare but he also has a large inheritance from his mother's side. She fled to Paris the minute France sold *Louisiane* 'cause she said the English language gives her an ear infection and Protestants make her rash. Her son was away studying at university but now he has returned to sell their plantation in *Vacherie.* Apparently, he's one of the wealthiest bachelors in all of New Orleans.

Beartrice   No wonder the gals swooned when he came to Mass late as a bowlegged harlot. Then had the nerve to sit in the colored section like he forgot he was white. Made Father Henri so upset he had a stuttering fit and kept saying 'Ha-ha-ha-ha-hail Mary' like he was sending us to hell instead of keeping us from it. I don't trust that boy; he's a rebel rouser.

La Veuve   Perhaps, but he'll be quite the catch at the masked ball tonight. The first *placée* to snare him will have a fine fortune on her hands. It might even be one of your daughters. God knows they're the most beautiful. *Très jolie.*

Beartrice   Who said my daughters was going? They're staying in the house for seven months to grieve like proper free colored women.

The daughters stop fanning.

La Veuve   My apologies, I just assumed Lazare would have wanted them to attend. This could be the last masked ball of their lives and considering their age and beauty – I figured it was ripe time they were picked. If you keep them in the house too long they could shrivel up or go mad. Speaking of which, how's your sister?

Everyone is stunned. Silence.

Beartrice   *Mes filles,* you may excuse yourselves. It's time for y'all to pick up the needle to embroider.

Odette   But *Maman*, we aren't finished with our tea.

Beartrice   Don't matter, too much tea dries your gut; gives you *flatulence.*

Agnès   But I thought you said it was good for mourning –

Maude Lynn   – and it dries our tears.

Beartrice *pounds her cane.*

Beartrice   ARE Y'ALL TALKING BACK?! You want to go to war with me?!

Agnès, Maude Lynn *and* **Odette**   *Non, Maman.*

Beartrice   Then retreat all of you . . . while you still got your lives.

They exit quickly into the parlor, followed by **Makeda**.

Agnès, Maude Lynn *and* **Odette**

(*singing*)	(*translation*)
Libera me, Domine,	*Deliver me, O Father,*
de morte aeterna	*from eternal death*
in die illa tremenda	*on that awful day*
quando coeli movendi	*when heaven and earth*
sunt et terra,	*shall be shaken*
dum veneris judicare	*and you shall come to*
saeculum per ignem.	*judge the world by fire.*
Tremens factus sum	*I am seized with fear*
ego et timeo,	*and trembling until the trial*
dum discussion venerit	*is at hand and the wrath*
atque venture ira:	*to come: when heavens*
Quando coeli movendi	*and earth shall be shaken.*
Sunt et terra.	

Makeda *and sisters enter their chamber.*

Agnès   Jesus, must she be so cruel? Sometimes I could just grab her by the hair and –

Makeda   Now, now, Agnès. She's still your mother. She loves you, she just has a hateful way of showing it.

Odette   If she loved us she'd let us attend the ball. There's only one a year and every quadroon from here to Hiawasee will be there but us. It's monstrous the way we're treated. We might as well be prisoners.

Maude Lynn   I don't mind it so. In fact, Jesus was a prisoner.

Odette   But Jesus wasn't a woman. He didn't have yearnings to fall in love like we have.

Agnès   Lord, and I have yearnings! I have burnings and yearnings. You have to help us, Makeda. You have a way with *Maman*. You have to convince her to let us go.

Makeda   I don't know, your mother seems set in her ways on this one.

Agnès   But you can move her; you're moving when you speak. You can stir her. *S'il te plait ma belle nounou.* Your voice . . .

She gives **Makeda** *a gold coin.*

Agnès   It's golden.

Makeda   Would you look at that.

She takes the coin and bites it.

My favorite flavor. I guess I could stir her a touch.

Agnès *and* **Odette**   *Merci beaucoup!*

They kiss **Makeda**, *who exits back into the tearoom where* **Beartrice** *and* **La Veuve** *are sitting.* **Makeda** *cleans.*

Beartrice   What you come here for, *Madame La Veuve?*

La Veuve   To pay my respects, of course.

Beartrice   Pay your respects to whom? You and Lazare wasn't close as far as I can recall and I know you don't like me, don't like nobody but the devil. You and him up to no good, coming in my house raisin Cain and rousing my daughters.

La Veuve   *Madame Albans*, you are mistaken. True: I've come here to pay more than my respects but my intentions are amicable. If you must know, folks are spreading terrible lies about you and I came here to . . . merely lay them at your feet.

Beartrice   That so? (*Sticks her feet out.*) Well, lay 'em.

La Veuve   For one, folks are wondering why you're so quick to start Lazare's wake. He died just this morn and already you got his body gutted and laid out for viewing. It's a bit unorthodox especially since you're not his wife.

Beartrice   Don't matter, I'll always be his true love. He spent most of his days at this house. He only married that miserable woman out of obligation – 'cause she's white and he needed to keep up appearances. Woman wouldn't even bear him any children. And when I told her Lazare had died, she danced a jig, poured a glass of champagne, kissed me on the lips and –

La Veuve   She kissed you on the lips?

Beartrice   Indeed. Then told me to dump his body in the river.

La Veuve   Still . . . folks are shocked he died so sudden. They say he looked healthy as a horse just last week.

Beartrice   He was seventy-two. You ever been seventy-two, *Madame La Veuve*? When you get there, let me know if you don't feel like dropping dead.

La Veuve   He's not the first lover of yours to die mysteriously though. Is he, *madame*?

Beartrice   A decent woman never talks about two things: her age and her lovers. You should know better, no wonder you can't keep a man.

La Veuve   I beg your pardon –

Beartrice   Course you do. When in doubt, do what you do best. Beg. But caution, men don't stay long with women who are always on their knees. Men want a woman whose face they can recognize in the street –

Makeda   Anybody for more praw-leans!

La Veuve   *Non*, I've had enough. It's gotten hot and I best get home. Makeda, you should come and see me soon, you look worn down. I have just the thing to lighten your load –

Beartrice   Makeda doesn't have time to be making house calls. She works for me.

La Veuve   I merely want to give her something, a token of my –

Beartrice   She don't have time to be your token! She's mine. Aren't you, Makeda?

Time.

Makeda   *Oui, madame.* My apologies. *ma'amzelle*, but I think it's best I stay close to home. But I thanks ya.

La Veuve   Well. No matter. Your house is going to fall anyway, Beartrice Albans. You may be the wealthiest colored woman in New Orleans but you built this house on sand, lies and dead bodies. Soon, it will lose its foundations and come crushing down on you like a cockroach under a boot. And then, God willing, I will have the sweet pleasure of clawing it from your hands and scraping you from the bottom of my sole. (*Sweet.*) *Adieu.*

Beartrice   Not if I do first.

La Veuve *exits.* **Makeda** *massages* **Beartrice***'s neck.*

Makeda   You must go slow, *madame.* This day will go long. You must breathe.

Beartrice   *Ah oui.*

Makeda   You must let things be . . . You must be at peace.

Beartrice   *Oui . . . mais oui . . .*

Makeda   You must . . . release . . . (*Beat.*) Release the girls for the ball —

Beartrice   What's this? Did they send you in here to stir me?

Makeda *stops.*

Makeda   *Non, madame,* I don't even have my spoon.

Beartrice   I don't care if Jesus comes to my door with a corsage, they're not going! Not ever! A mother must keep her young close living in this town full of snakes. Some hiss, others gnash their teeth, but tomorrow, they will all crawl from the grass and stretch out full-grown to bite down on us and taste our blood. We must bear their stings with a cold beauty and indestructible grace. We will only go out on holidays, we will speak with pearly smiles and present our passports like jewels when we have to prove our freedom. We will sit in the colored sections proudly and whisper curses only in French. We will lay low among these vipers and yet hold our heads high, for this is how women endure war. They nest. And we will nest here until we sigh our final breath. *Compris?*

Makeda   *Oui, madame.*

Beartrice   Monsieur Pomeray, Lazare's lawyer, will be around shortly to show me the will and give me the deed to this house. This place will shield us. In this house we'll all be free.

Makeda   Not me. What about me? You said you'd set me free soon as you got the deed. You said you'd give me my papers, 'member?

Beartrice   Course. I haven't forgot. (*Beat.*) Just sad you sound so eager to leave, I figured us for family.

Makeda   *Non*, I'm your house servant. I wants my freedom. I ain't gettin no younger.

Beartrice   I see. Well, the girls will shed more than a few tears to hear you're leaving them. (*Referring to her massage.*) Now please . . . continue.

Makeda   *Oui madame.* Now bow your head –

She massages. We return to the daughters:

Agnès   My eyes were closed in prayer, my arms folded across the pew, when suddenly I heard a pair of boots pause just in front of me. I opened my eyes, looked up, and there he was – Ràmon Le Pip: with lips pink as posies and eyes green as the sea. He looked at me like I was the Last Supper and said . . . (*Deep voice.*) *Salut.*

Maude Lynn   Dear God!

Odette   *Silence*, Maude Lynn, *Maman* will hear us! Keep going, Agnès, and talk slow, it's getting good . . .

Agnès   Once he caught my eyes, it felt like he entered my body and was walking round inside me. Kissing the back of my mouth, sliding down my throat . . . Laying his head in the deep caverns of my bountiful bosom. Just the smell of his hot, sweaty breath on my face made me . . . dewy.

Maude Lynn   Jesus keep me near the cross.

Agnès   I felt spring! In the delta regions of my womanness and sprung the coolest pond between my legs, then sighed. That's when he grinned. As if he knew just by speaking to me, he had made me come to Jesus –

Maude Lynn   BLASPHEMY!

Odette *covers* **Maude Lynn**'*s mouth.*

Agnès   Right there, in my seat. Just by looking deep into me, he saw desire and plucked it. Then grinned like a cat who just cornered a mouse.

Odette   And what you do? What did you do then? Did you smile back?

Agnès   *Non*, I'm Catholic, I wanted him to suffer. So I bit my lip. Bit it so hard I drew blood then licked it. Like a finger pressed over scripture: I moved my tongue slowly cross the pages of my mouth, across the blood, and when I got to the end, I whispered . . . *(Soft.) Selah.*

Odette   And what he do? What he do then? Did he whisper back?

Agnès   *Non.* Instead he ripped out two pages in a church hymnal and wrote me a letter with ink from his pocket. I hid the letter between my breasts and haven't read it fully for fear *Maman* will get a hold of it. Do me a favor and read it to me, Odette. Read it slow, sis, and with the diction of an elocutionist.

She hands the letter to **Odette**.

Odette (*reading with a French accent*)   *Chère,*

You made more than my heart sing the minute I saw your face.

And alas, what fate to find you in the last place I'd ever thought I'd be —

A church.

I must admit I don't read the holy writ nor am I the holy kind.

I only came to church to taste the communion wine.

Yet my thirst was quenched when I saw you lick your lips.

Spread your thighs like Moses parting the sea.

Spend the rest of your life with me?

Oui, I'm crazy but so are the stars.

For they speak in sparkles just as our eyes did — love at first light.

Meet me tonight, at the ball.

I may be a fool, but don't make a fool of God above.

He wants to make a believer out of you and me.

He wants us to fall in love.

Je t'embrasse, Ràmon Le Pip.

(*Her own voice.*) Oh my, he sounds lovely, Agnès. Like he walked out of a dream.

Maude Lynn   Dream or not, you better wake up. God's watching you and writing what you do in His book. When you get to the pearly gates first thing St. Peter gone do is read your mess. 'And Ràmon ripped two pages in a hymnal in the House of God and wrote Agnès a letter like she was a harlot. And verily she became one when she took that letter and put it between her breasts.'

Agnès   Get thee to a nunnery, Maude Lynn.

Odette   I think it's romantic.

Agnès   Thank you, Odette.

Odette   I think you're going to hell for putting two ripped pages from a church hymnal between your breasts, but it's still romantic.

Agnès   That's because I was meant for romance and frivolous escapades and I will wait no longer. My body is aching for Ràmon Le Pip and I intend to set it free tonight at the ball.

Odette   So you really think Makeda can convince *Maman* to let us go?

Agnès   *Non, maman* is unmovable. I only gave Makeda that task to keep her busy. I'm going to do what I planned to do all along, I'm going to sneak out.

Maude Lynn   How do you plan to do that? Even if you could manage to get pass *Maman*, you still need her to escort you and negotiate your price. No woman in history has ever become a man's *placée* without their mother's consent.

Agnès   Maybe so, but it's a masked ball. If I can convince someone to slip out of the house with me and pretend to be *Maman*, I could pull it off.

Odette *and* **Maude Lynn** *make eyes.*

Agnès   All they'd have to do is dress up, mask their face and, once I find Ràmon, they'd negotiate my price and sign my papers. It'll be easy as jumping rope.

Maude Lynn   Till *Maman* find out and whip you with one. Count me out, butt beatins don't do nothing pretty for my skin.

Agnès   And who needs you, I got my favorite sis. Odette, you'll come to the ball and pretend to be *Maman* for me, won't you? You got a heart like me. You and me, we men-lovers: we love us some men. But if we don't follow where our hearts lead, we will end up like Taunte Marie and go mad.

Enter **Marie Josephine**, *forty, on to the back porch dressed in a
white, cotton nightgown, an old, tattered tutu, a silk scarf and red
sandals. Her hair hangs like vines and she wears an elaborate tignon
made up of a coo-coo bird in a nest eating dry, exotic fruit.*

Marie Josephine (*singing*)
   When tulips form a crown . . .
   Spin them round
   Till the moon goes down.

Agnès   If you help me, Odette, if you give me wings, I will fly
like a bird. But if you don't, I won't risk the leap and will
be forced to stay here, on the edge of this world, lost forever.
Silently screaming for Ràmon Le Pip, who, on the other side,
shall never hear my chirp. You must give me wings, sis.

She extends her hand for a shake. **Odette** *looks at* **Maude Lynn**.

Maude Lynn   Once you shake hands with the devil, count
your fingers.

Odette   I'll do it. But on one condition: you must promise to
tell *Maman* that this was your idea. You must tell her that this
was your scheme, Agnès. Promise?

Agnès   *Oui. Je promesse.*

She shakes **Odette**'s *hand then twirls her into a waltz. Below,*
Marie Josephine *dances with an invisible beau.*

Marie Josephine (*singing a waltz*)
   Ladies gather round
   Dripping moonlight from their gowns
   Long-sleeve gloves and garlands and tulips form a crown.
   Spin them round, spin them round,
   Spin those ladies all over town,
   Till the moon goes down/

   Come to the hall
   Masked to enthrall
   You'll have a ball
   With the Vienesse waltz.

Toss off your shawls
Orchestra calls
You'll have a ball
With the Vienesse waltz.

Step la-la. Step la-la. Step la-la. Step.
Turn tra-la. Turn tra-la. Turn tra-la 'gain
Quick step and lock step but keep your distance
Cross step to box step and grab you a man!

Marie Josephine *waltzes by herself.*

Marie Josephine, Agnès, Maude Lynn *and* **Odette**
Step la-la. Step la-la. Step la-la. Step.
Turn tra-la. Turn tra-la. Turn tra-la 'gain
Quick step and lock step but keep your distance
Cross step to box step and grab you a man!

Agnès, Maude Lynn *and* **Odette**
Toss off your shawls
Orchestra calls
You'll have a ball
With the Vienesse waltz.

The girls fall on to the bed laughing. Downstairs, **Beartrice** *pounds her cane.*

Beartrice   Silence that noise! You're supposed to be in mourning!

Agnès, Maude Lynn *and* **Odette**   *Oui, Maman.*

Enter **Makeda**.

Makeda   Your visitor is here, *madame. Monsieur Pomeray,* Lazare's lawyer, I sat him in the sitting room.

Beartrice   *Merci. Dieu merci!*

Below, **Marie Josephine** *lifts cloth from the body.*

Marie Josephine   Lazare? Lazare, why you sleepin on the dining room table? You know my sister gone have your neck when she finds you here.

She puts her ear to his mouth.

Dead? What you mean you dead? (*Beat.*) Oh, *pauvre*! *Pauvre.*
Poor Lazare.

Beartrice   What's that wailing? Sounds like somebody
skinning a cat.

Makeda   It's your sister.

Beartrice   Hurry and put her in her room before *Monsieur
Pomeray* sees her. That's all I need, more folks spreadin gossip
'bout me and my household. She wanna croon, put her in the
slave quarters with the roosters.

Makeda *hurries into the parlor as* **Beartrice** *exits into the sitting
room.* **Marie Josephine** *cries over the dead body.*

Marie Josephine   *Pauvre* Lazare. Poor, po Lazare!

Makeda   He died this morning, Marie. Was going tell you
earlier but you been sleep most of the day.

Marie Josephine   Beartrice killed him!

Makeda   Shh. She's in the sitting room. Your sister's a bear
but she's no murderer. 'Sides Dr Phillipe said Lazare died of a
heart attack.

Marie Josephine   And what Dr Phillipe know? He
diagnosed me as crazy so you know he ain't wrapped too tight.
She killed him. Lazare told me himself. Even though he dead
me and him still on speaking terms. The dead got much
power. Most folks don't want to believe it 'cause it don't make
natural sense but I got six cents.

She shows six pennies in her hand.

And that affords me just enough to hear what most folks can't.
Lazare say his spirit gone sit on the roof till it caves in and
crushes Beartrice to dust. He also say he hungry and he wants
to know if you can fix him some meat.

Makeda *rolls her eyes, doubtful, then suddenly a chair moves by itself. Silence. In the bedroom:*

Maude Lynn   I'm famished, I'm going downstairs to get supper.

Agnès   Supper ain't till dusk. Why you leavin so early?

Maude Lynn   'Cause I'm hungry. I haven't eaten since breakfast.

Agnès   I don't believe you. Odette quick, block the door.

Odette *does so.*

Maude Lynn   What's this?

Agnès   I'm not letting you leave this room, Maude Lynn Albans. You got a mouth the size of the Mississippi and a tongue that moves faster than green grass through a goose. I know you want to tell *Maman* that we're sneaking to the ball but, as God is my witness, if you try and leave or scream, I will beat you till you rope like okra. Do we have an understanding?

Maude Lynn   I understand that you done lost what's left of your Godforsaken mind.

In the parlor:

Marie Josephine   I ain't crazy. She killed him like she killed the first, I just didn't tell nobody 'cause she my sister and it's bad luck to stab your sister in the back. It'll cause the whole family to bleed. That's why I can't tell a soul.

Makeda   Then don't.

Marie Josephine   Fine, you forced my hand. Thirty years ago, Beartrice fell in love with a white sugar farmer named Armand DuPless. They met at a quadroon ball and it was love at first waltz. Till Beartrice came home one Sunday and heard Armand making body music in the bedroom with another woman. Sister was so mad she spit blood, but dared not make a scene for she was Armand's *placée*, not his wife. So she swallowed her pride, bit her lip and cracked open the door to steal a peek. That's when she discovered that the newfound

lover was her dearest friend, *Madame* La Veuve. Now sister was
so mad she chewed her teeth. She thought of breaking down
the door and pouring hot jambalaya on their naked bodies,
she thought of taking her paring knife and cutting both of
their throats while they slept, but violence was beneath her.
Sister is cold, callous, malicious and mean but she's still a lady.
So she left the house and plotted all night. She knew that if she
waited too long, Armand would make La Veuve his *placée*;
sister would be cut off financially and her reputation ruined.
So Beartrice did what any wise Creole woman would have
done in 1806. She baked Armand a sweet potato pie. (*Beat.*)
They never found his body. And when she was questioned
about his disappearance and the money that was left her in his
will, she weaved such a tight-knit story that the authorities
threw up their hands and tied an inconclusive knot around the
whole affair.

Upstairs: **Agnès** *and* **Odette** *are dressed. They tie* **Maude Lynn**
to a chair with rope.

Maude Lynn   Go 'head, tie me up! This just how the
Romans did Jesus. He tried to keep folks from the fiery pit but
they didn't listen to Him either. So go ahead, tie me! It don't
matter that I'm your sister: Jesus' people turned on Him too. It
don't matter that I'm starving: Jesus fasted forty days and forty
nights. It don't even matter that you're tying me so tight I can
hardly breathe: Jesus bled to death! O Father, forgive my sisters
for they know not what I'm a do when I get up from here.

Below:

Marie Josephine   Lazare won't sit idle. All the bad deeds
Beartrice did in life are finally coming home to roost. Lazare
say he gone push down on this house till it won't stand.

Makeda   The *maître* sho doing a lot of talking for a dead man.

Marie Josephine   Course. What else a ghost got to do
when it get stuck but bump its gums? When a spirit comes to
the end of its journey it's faced with a door. The door of its
soul. Some say it leads to heaven, some say hell, others say it

be the way to your next life. In any case, a spirit don't have to go through that door if it don't want. It can stay stuck. It can be a ghost. Like take me and you – we stuck. Stuck in this house. We both see the front door every day and we know there's another life on the other side but we choose not to go through it. 'Cause we stuck. Beartrice got us chained.

Makeda   Speak for yourself. I found me a way out. Just today your sister said she'd sign my papers as soon as she gets the deed from Lazare's lawyer. I don't know about you but I'm gonna be free.

Marie Josephine   Sth. You're too old to be a fool. The only way you leaving this place is over Beartrice's dead body and just so you know, neither God nor the devil is man enough to take her. I tried many times to get out. More times than there are ticks in a clock, but sister always manages to keep me in her little hands. (*Whispering.*) I used to have a man on the outside who'd be waiting for me. He was a Negro drummer – black as shut-eye. I used to sneak out and meet him at dawn on Sundays at Congo Square and dance with him till the moon climbed out of the skirts of the Mississippi. Every Sunday he'd beat my name into his drum and it'd sing: *Marie, Marie.* Till one morn, Beartrice caught me trying to leave and the hag locked me in my room for seven months. When I finally got free, it was too late. Folks said my drummer had died from the consumption. Died with his arms wrapped around his drum. The news broke me into tears. It made my mind go soft and my heart wild. Sometimes I think I hear him though, at dusk. I hear his drum calling me. Makes me think, his spirit is still in this world and he stuck too, waiting for me before he goes through his soul's door. And I think for a mere tick . . . that it's my time to get.

Makeda   That's 'cause it is. It's time for you to get your rump in your room.

She shoves her in the room as **Marie Josephine** *secretly steals the keys from* **Makeda**'s *pocket. In the bedroom:* **Agnès** *combs* **Odette**'s *hair.* **Maude Lynn**'s *tied up, prays.*

Odette   I don't feel right locking her in here, Agnès. She looks sad.

Agnès   Naw she don't, that's just her look.

Odette   But don't you feel awful? We're steppin on the heart of own our sister, just so we can dance at the ball.

Agnès   *Non*, I'm the one dancin. You're walkin 'round chitin chattin, carryin on, pretendin to be *Maman*, remember? Let's stay focused.

Odette   Course. How can I forget. Tonight's about you.

Agnès   Now you preachin. And don't look so blue, I'll find y'all beau too. Once you sign me and Ràmon's papers as *Maman*, I'll see to it that Ràmon introduces you to one of his male acquaintances and later perhaps I'll introduce Maude Lynn to one of his cousins or an older altar boy who don't mind being nagged half to death.

Odette   You will?

Agnès   Course, I'm sweet like that.

Odette   Oh, Agnès, that would be wonderful. Then I wouldn't have to stay in this costume and people could see me: they could see my beauty.

Agnès   Your beauty!? Hold on, you keep gettin beside yourself and into my light, sis. Tonight's about me, remember? I'm the oldest. *I'm* the beauty. You need to stay in the shadows; keep a lookout.

Odette   Oh, course. I keep forgettin. (*Rehearsing*) Tonight's . . . about you.

Agnès   Good girl, now we must hurry. I feel *mon père*'s spirit pushing me, urging me to leave this house. We're Creoles, for crying out loud. A life of imprisonment is better suited for slaves.

Odette   *Maman* say being a *placée* ain't much different from being a slave.

Agnès   *Maman* is a hypocrite. She would be nothing if she wasn't a *placée*. So what if they are bought for a price? At least they're worth something.

Odette   But why let someone tell you your worth? I know my worth and it's priceless. No man will ever tag me.

Agnès   Don't be a fool, you a gal and you're colored.

Odette   *Oui* and so are you.

Agnès   Of course, but I'm fair. You're colored brown. If you were my hue or lighter, maybe you could put on airs, but let's face it, you were born with the family stain, Odette. You'd be lucky to be a *placée*.

Odette   What do you mean . . . family stain?

Maude Lynn   Agnès, be soft, she's just a babe. *Maman* will skin you if you say too much.

Odette   Say too much of what? Agnès, what is she talking about? (*Beat.*) Agnès?!

Agnès   No one's told you the truth 'cause they didn't want to hurt you, but since we're going out into the grown-up world, I figure it's time you became a woman. You're dark, Odette. You've got more brown than the paper bag. This means you wear the stain in our blood that we so desperately try to hide. *Mo chagren ma chère*, you are beautiful: you have the most beautiful hair eyes have ever seen, but you are black. And that means you have no choice in life – you're at the bottom. In fact, you'd be blessed if a white man even looked at you.

Odette *looks into a mirror, (the audience). She applies powder to her face as she hums.* **Marie Josephine** *has snuck out of her room. She talks to* **Lazare***'s corpse.*

Marie Josephine
My man who plays the *bamboulas* is black as good night
With eyes that keep the shimmer of stars
And muscles thick as ice. He quenches the summer heat
With lips: deep purple as jasmine spice

His kiss be the only way to Paradise.
I loved him once and hard
So hard it took my mind only a second to go soft
I got lost in his arms, which held me so tight
Like tides in a sea of "never let me go." I went
To the market to buy *un chapeau*
And saw him drumming in *Place Congo*
"Dance," he said. "*Calinda*.
I massage these beats on this drum for your back,
For your arms to take wing. For your head to go back . . .
There. 'Member . . . when you was my Queen, *ma chère?*"
"*Non*," I answered. "I'm not black."
He laughed with teeth so white the light could make you
    blind. He said,
"The drum told me you were mine.
I can see past your skin and the lies they put in your head.
We were divine way back when
Let me be your King again."
"But what will my father say, how will my mother survive
    the shame.
I was born to be a white man's *placée* . . . "
"No Marie, you were born to just be."
And that's when he kissed me
Filled my mind with history denied me
And I danced.

She dances. Suddenly, a wind blows and raps at the window.

Lazare, is that you? What you mean, you getting ready to
bring down the roof? But what about the girls? Who's gonna
get them out?

In the bedroom, **Agnès** *dresses* **Odette**.

Agnès   You don't look enough like *Maman*, Odette. You need
stuffing.

She gives **Odette** *the once-over.*

Agnès   First, you need more bosom. *Maman* got sacks for
days. Open.

She stuffs cloth in **Odette**'*s bodice.*

Agnès   Next you need more gut. *Maman* got enough belly to rub a wish from. Lift.

She stuffs a pillow in **Odette**'*s corset.*

Agnès   Finally, you need more rump. *Maman* can literally put her butt on her shoulders. Turn round.

She stuffs two ring pillows up the back of **Odette**'*s dress.*

Agnès   *Bon.* Now you ready for the ball. Go and stuff Maude Lynn in case she decides to scream on our way out.

She hands **Odette** *a handkerchief.*

Maude Lynn   Please, don't stuff me, Odette. I won't tell a soul. Just let me keep my mouth.

Odette   What if she can't breathe, Agnès?

Agnès   She nosey, she can breathe through her nose. Stuff her!

Odette *stuffs her. In the parlor:* **Makeda** *finds* **Beartrice** *sitting on her throne, looking over the will.*

Makeda   You look like you got something that wants to crawl out of your mouth but you don't want to spit it. I don't mind spit, *madame.* Even an elegant lady got to spit every now and then if only to clear her throat. You can clear your throat with me, if you want. I won't tell nobody.

Beartrice   Why you barking up my tree, Makeda? You see a bone in my bush?

Makeda   *Non,* no reason. Just kinda itchy to hear what the lawyer said. Been thinking 'bout it all day. Can't hardly sit still 'cause my hands are aching to grab hold and touch my freedom. It's so close I can taste it. Tell me, *s'il vous plait,* did Lazare leave you that deed in his will?

Beartrice   Course. Course he did.

Makeda   Sweet Jesus! I'm going to be free!

In the distance, **Agnès** *and* **Odette** *sneak out of the house.* **Marie Josephine** *watches them exit.*

Beartrice   But I didn't get nothing.

Makeda   Come 'gain?

Beartrice   Nothing: that's what I got. Didn't matter that he left me the deed, wrote my name all over the will. That he gave me every penny he had and confessed in the blackest ink that I was his true love. Didn't matter 'cause the laws have already changed and I'm colored. And, according to US law, a colored mistress can't be given assets over a white widow. Even if it's writ in the deceased's will. Even if he has children with the colored mistress and none with the wife. The widow still gets everything 'cause her skin is the real currency and mine seems to be losing value as the days go by. She gets everything: the house, Lazare's businesses, his boats, she even gets the cat. Which means I have nothing.

Makeda   You got to fight her, *madame.* You got to keep what's rightfully yours. You're Beartrice Albans; people revere you. New Orleans will stand on your shoulders.

Beartrice   The law is clear. It was made to serve and protect a certain few, but, make no mistake, she's not getting this house. I'm going to have to convince her to let me keep it.

Makeda   And how are you gonna do that?

Beartrice   Easy. I'm going to make her a sweet potato pie.

In the bedroom, **Maude Lynn** *prays.* **Marie Josephine** *makes her way to the room.*

Maude Lynn   I don't want to die, Jesus. I thought I could be a martyr like you but I don't have the gut for it. It was precious at first but now my stomach is grumbling and Lord . . . I got to make more water than Delta flood. Now the Bible say, "Ask and it shall be given unto you; seek and you will find, knock and the door – "

A knock.

Jesus? (*Beat.*) Thank ya, Jesus. (*Calling*) Help me, I'm locked in here!

Marie Josephine   Who dat?

Maude Lynn   Ta Ta? Taunte Marie, it's me. It's ya Maude Lynn.

Marie Josephine   O, my crybaby. Gal, I come to set you and ya sisters free. Just hold ya thighs.

She picks the door lock with the hatpin.

Come on, you free as a bird, babe!

Maude Lynn *embraces her aunt.*

Maude Lynn   God bless ya, Tauntie. You a savior. My sisters done snuck out the house and went to the ball.

Marie Josephine   Wonderful.

Maude Lynn   *Non*, I have to tell *Maman*.

Marie Josephine   *Ne fais pas ça, ma chère,* don't tell on your sisters. If you stab them in the back, the whole family will bleed. Come with me! We must get free. We must leave this house now!

Maude Lynn   I can't, I said! I have to tell *Maman*! I have to save them. It's for their own good!

Marie Josephine *grabs her and tries to prevent her from telling. They tussle. In the tearoom,* **Beartrice** *prepares to leave.*

Makeda   Been working in your house twenty years and I ain't seen you so much as butter a biscuit let alone bake a pie. If the pie that good, you'd think you make it more often.

Beartrice   I only serve it when somebody's really hungry.

Makeda   Heard you served it to your first love. Heard it sent him to heaven.

Beartrice   Yeah, but I'm not one to boast. It's a family recipe.

Makeda   Mercy! So you just proud of killin white folks?

Beartrice   *Excuse moi!*

Makeda   You don't think they gone find you out, *madame?*
They gone hang you like a shot-up hat.

Beartrice   Gal, what is you talking about?

Makeda   I'm talking 'bout your pies! Your sister told me
how they put folks in the ground. She say you gave one to your
first love for fear of being cut off financially and ever since
then nobody can find his body. And now you getting ready to
serve that same sort of pie to Lazare's widow and I can't let you
do it. As bad as I want to be free, I can't let you kill another
white for money. It just ain't of Jesus.

Beartrice   My pie ain't poisonous, Makeda. It's *my* pie. My
sweet pie. The pie God gave me, *compris?*

Time. She finally understands.

Makeda   Oh.

Beartrice   What I look like serving folks poisonous pies and
I can barely cook. Use your head and stop listen to the
ramblings of a mad woman. My sister hates me 'cause I won't
let her roam the streets and will spin any story to fit her lunacy.
I didn't kill my first. He was having an affair with my dearest
friend at the time so I gave him enough pie to make him
lovesick. Fed him my goods all day and night till the poor fool
lost his mind. He became lustful, started acting jealous, didn't
want me leaving the house. Just wanted to eat me up. It got so
bad that I had to leave him and the man killed himself. My pie
is that good.

Makeda   Ain't nobody's pie that good?

Beartrice   Mine is. And Lazare's wife knows it, that's why
she wants a piece. She wants what every man has wanted from
me all my life – my flesh. I figure it's my cross and my salvation.
But I'll bear it. If it means my gals can have shelter, she can do
what she wants to me.

Makeda   Ain't this some world? You wouldn't have to do this, *madame*, if you let your daughters go to that ball.

Beartrice   I'm not going down this road with you again, Makeda –

Makeda   If just one of them became a *placée*, you would be set for life. You could pay the wife off, keep the house and give me my freedom –

Beartrice   Being a *placée* is slavery!

Makeda   It's life! You're too stubborn to see it but we're women. None of us are born free. We got to beg, borrow and steal just to make a place. There ain't no other way –

Beartrice   There's my way! And as long as you're under my roof that's how it's gonna be. I will not, in this life or the next, sell my daughters into this world!

Maude Lynn   It's too late, *Maman*, they're gone.

Enter **Maude Lynn** *followed by* **Marie Josephine**.

Maude Lynn   They snuck out. I tried to get to you, to tell you, but they tied me up and by now . . . Odette has got Agnès sold.

Beartrice   What's this?! They disobeyed me? Snuck out and betrayed their own mother?! And after I been breaking my back to keep 'em, save 'em! They went and disobeyed *me*! Well, heaven help 'em! 'CAUSE NOW I GOT TO RAISE HELL!

She pounds her cane. The house shakes. Candlelights flicker. A picture falls off the wall and the window shutters rap as if moved by a strong wind. The clocks turn on and chime, black crêpe falls from the windows and in the mirrors we see faces of ancestors past. Then a moan. **Beartrice** *looks at the audience.*

Beartrice (*as if chewing nails*)   Lazare.

Lights fade to black.

End of Act One.

Act Two

Three hours later, night squats over the cottage like a raven cruising for hunt. We hear the midnight song of New Orleans: crickets greasing their legs, cats fucking the flesh off of each other, frogs burping zydeco and a drunk crooning about High John de Conqueror. A pink-eyed full moon pours shafts of smoky light into random corners of the tearoom where the following women sit in a half circle around the corpse. **Makeda** *kneels, lights a candle before her altar,* **Maude Lynn**, *prays,* **Marie** *shakes a rattle and* **Beartrice** *recites the Apostle's Creed while smoking a cigar.*

Makeda (*offering to the four winds, smoking a cigar*)

Spirit of the Ifá
I call on you.
Spirit of Pap' Legba,
Bless this house.

She blows smoke over a rock.

Clear all obstacles
In our path,
Will you?
Papa Legba
bless this house

She sprinkles water over the rock.

Makeda (*spoken*)
What can we do, Papa
To get rid of this haunt?
Help us
Tell me what I should do?

She tosses cowrie shells on the floor. She reads them.

Beartrice (*reading*)
I believe in God the Father Almighty. Maker of heaven and earth: And in Jesus Christ His only Son our Lord, Who was conceived by the Holy Ghost, Born of the Virgin Mary: Suffered under Pontius Pilate, Was crucified, dead, and buried: He descended into hell. The third day He rose again from the dead; He ascended into heaven, and sitteth on the right hand of God the Father Almighty. From thence He shall come to judge the quick and the dead. I believe in the Holy Ghost; The holy Catholic church; the Communion of Saints; The Forgiveness of sins; The resurrection of the body, And the Life everlasting. Amen.

The house shakes! **Lazare** *rises.* **Maude Lynn** *screams.*

Beartrice   Everybody be still.

Lazare *examines his old body.*

Lazare   Does anybody feel a draft?

Maude Lynn   *Mon père?*

She walks toward him.

Beartrice   Maude Lynn, I said be still.

Maude Lynn   *Mon père*, is that you?

Lazare   *Oui. Venez-ici, mon chou.* Let your *père* kiss ya.

Maude Lynn *runs into his arms.*

Maude Lynn   Glory to God! It's you in the flesh! But what are you?

Lazare   I'm spirit, babe. You believe in spirits, don't you?

Maude Lynn   The Holy Spirit, but you don't look holy. Have you come from heaven or did they raise you from hell?

Lazare   Neither. Neither horn nor halo has crowned this head. I was in a limbo: a dream. Floating on a river in the deepest deep when I saw a light from a candle curl into a wagging finger. It beckoned me, called me out of darkness and rocked me back into my bones, wrapped me in this flesh. And now I'm here. Half alive and tired. I've gotten no rest, babe.

Beartrice   They say there's none for the wicked.

Lazare (*as if eating shit*)   *Mop tee.* Shoulda known you'd be here.

Beartrice   You more trouble dead then you was alive, Lazare.

He tries to snatch her but he stumbles.

Lazare   You want to come join me!

Makeda   Don't move *maître*, your body's half rotten and we only have a little time.

Lazare   Well, it took ya long enough. I been tryin to get y'all attention for hours. Been movin furniture, shakin the house like loose change. But I'm back now. *Makeed*, be a good girl and light me a *cigare*.

Makeda   *Oui, maître –*

Beartrice   Makeda, don't move. You don't take orders from him.

Lazare   How come she don't? This still my house. You do as I say, Makeda.

Makeda *does not move. Time.*

Lazare   Well, don't this feed the chickens. A man ain't been dead a day and already the women in his house got on his pants. Marie?!

Marie Josephine   *Oui, frère.*

Lazare   Bring me a bottle of my best wine. If they won't give me a smoke, I'm certainly gonna drink.

Marie Josephine   I'll get two glasses.

Beartrice   Marie, you stay right there!

Marie Josephine   Don't sass me, sis. *I'll* go as I please now. I can hear the ticks. I'm getting free.

She exits for the wine.

Maude Lynn   Ain't no cause to stir up trouble now, *père*. Tell us why you hauntin us. Tell us why you won't rest.

Lazare   I got unfinished business. And a good businessman settles all his accounts. He counts his chicks before they hatch and kills the fox before she lures him away with her tail. I got lured –

Beartrice   He's talking nonsense. He's a ghost! He can't throw his weight around no more so he's tossing lies.

Lazare   I've come back to save my chicks! I come to make sure they all take flight. Just look around, babe, this house is becoming a casket. The walls are closing in, the roof saggin low. Do you want to wither in here like your aunt? Your mother is going to suffocate you in her arms. Trust me. I let her creep into my heart, take my gals then take my life −

Beartrice   We done put up with you long enough, Lazare! Wash him off our backs, Makeda. It's time for him to get.

Makeda *drinks water and spits it at* **Lazare**, *who recoils. The water burns him.*

Lazare   *AHHH! Non!* I'm not leaving! Not leaving till I get my girls free.

Marie Josephine *enters.*

Beartrice   We ain't got time for that.

Maude Lynn   *Maman*, you're hurting him.

Lazare   Let me speak first!

Marie Josephine   Let him speak, Beartrice! Let the dead say their piece!

Beartrice   We don't have time! More water, Makeda!

Maude Lynn   Let him speak first, *Maman*! Please!

Makeda *swallows ore water for spitting.* **Maude Lynn** *stands to protect him.*

Marie Josephine   Ooo, *bon*. Here it comes. Truth. It comes home late but it's always on time.

Lazare   She killed me.

Marie Josephine   There it is.

Beartrice   Dr Phillipe said you died of a heart attack.

Lazare   What Dr Phillipe know. The man said I was a drunk, so you know he ain't altogether upstairs. Tell them the truth, *mop tee*! Tell them what you whispered in my ear. Tell them how it turned my heart so cold it froze into ice. Tell them how you put roots on me for months: cuttin pieces of my hair when I was asleep, shakin bones over my shoes, putting blood in my coffee.

Beartrice   Those were protection spells. I wouldn't take that long to kill nobody. I don't have the patience.

Maude Lynn   But *Maman*, you're Catholic. You know better than having your hand in a black bag. It's witchcraft.

Makeda   It's my faith. And it's healed you more than once when you was a gal, Maude Lynn.

Lazare   Don't let her rosary beads fool you. Every Creole woman in this city know a touch hoo doo.

Beartrice   He's just tryin to twist your head against me.

Marie Josephine   Not me. My head's already twisted. I'm already against ya.

Maude Lynn   *Maman*, is it true?

Beartrice   I don't have to answer to nobody. Only the head can look back at the tail.

Marie Josephine   Tell the truth then, sis! It's ripe time.

Lazare   Tell 'em!

Makeda   *Madame?*

Maude Lynn   *Maman*, please –

Beartrice   He was going to force my girls to be *placées*! He was going to give them to more men like him.

Lazare   It's what they were raised for.

Beartrice   It nearly killed me. Having to be some man's thing. Most of my life – having to be a mule in a dress. I couldn't do it to my daughters. Told him so, begged him, but he tried to make me bend to his will. After twenty years! Putting up with his drunken fits, nursing him to health, tolerating his wife, seeing to his house, his businesses, feeding him like a babe, he was going to put my daughters in chains and I couldn't do it. Wouldn't.

Lazare   You're no slave. You chose to be a *placée*. I never forced you. You wanted it: the gowns, the gold, the house –

Beartrice   I wanted a piece of life!

Lazare   And you got a big piece!

Beartrice   What other choice a colored woman got?! I crawled my way up from nothing and with the help of no one. All my days – on my knees begging, bowing.

Lazare *(sweet)*   You had it easy, I gave you your heart's desire –

Beartrice   Just as long as I opened my legs and kept my mouth shut! But a woman gets tired, Lazare. She gets old and then she gets wise. I had had enough. Last night, with his hands around my throat, I looked in his eyes and saw the reflection of my girls. I peered into the future and saw them in tears, wailing. Each of them separated from the other: one run off, one living with and feeding the poor, the last sullen, hiding her face from daylight. I couldn't bear it. Couldn't bear to see them in pain, so I decided to live. With his hands around my throat, I mustered just enough strength to turn my head to his ear and whisper a black magic song. It stole his last breath.

Lazare *remembers, touches his heart.*

Beartrice   It was either me or him. And for once, I chose myself.

She sits, finally free of her guilt.

Maude Lynn   You're going to hell, *Maman.* (*To* **Lazare**.) Both of you: headed to the fiery pit and I hope the devil chain you two together.

She exits.

Lazare   Maude Lynn!

He starts after her.

Beartrice   Let her be. Her heart just needs to have a long chat with her head.

Lazare (*to* **Beartrice**)   You turned her against me! You turned all my gals against me! But it won't do you no good. This my *maison*. And I ain't leavin till I bring down the roof!

Makeda   Oh no you ain't. I ain't cleanin up after folks once they die. A Negro woman's got to draw the line somewhere. It's time for you to pack your soul and get to wherever you got to get.

She continues the ritual.

Lazare   I said I ain't leavin till I'm ready! Till I put my full weight on this house and come tumbling on *mop tee*'s pretty little head.

Marie Josephine   Be good, Lazare. If you do that, you'll kill us all.

Lazare   No, my fall won't be made of bricks and stones! I'm comin with darkness. I'm bringing years, decades of the dark and utter quiet!

Beartrice   Makeda, usher him back to the dark. I done had enough of this. If Lazare won't leave my house, he'll at least leave my sight.

Makeda *kneels near her candle. She covers herself in white chalk then hands it to the others who cover themselves – all save **Maude Lynn**.* **Makeda** *sprinkles water on **Lazare**'s feet. It sizzles and he hops away from her.*

Lazare   Why you do her dirty work? She's never going to give you your freedom. You will always be her slave, Makeed. Wasn't I good to you, gal? You hear what I say?! Didn't we have a time? (*Beat.*) Makeed!!?

Lazare *is almost swallowed by darkness*

Marie Josephine   (*to* **Lazare**) Guess this is goodbye. I wanted her to go easier on you but Beartrice swears there's only one way to deal with a bad ghost and that's to be bad. Most ghosts is stubborn. I'll still try and get the girls to leave but . . . it sho be nice if you took the first step, Lazare.

Lazare *starts to exit, but stops.*

Lazare   Sis? There's somebody lookin for you. In the spirit world. He black, dark as a night with no stars, eyes like moon, teeth white as eggshell. He's a drummer. He say he play the *bamboulas.*

Marie Josephine *covers her mouth, her body shakes.*

Lazare   He been lookin so long for you, they say the only song he'll sing is your name. He wants you to meet him at Congo Square in the morn just before the sun rises from the Mississippi. He say that's the only way you're going to see him and he see you, and you hear his drum.

He exits but not through the door.

Makeda (*singing*)
    Spririt of Iya,
    I thank you.
    Spirit of Pa Hegba
    Clear a path for him too

Makeda *kneels before the altar again. She sprinkles water on the rock, then kisses the ground.*

Marie Josephine   Y'all hear that? He been waiting. I knew it. My man been waiting in the spirit world for me all this time.

Beartrice   Don't get beside yourself, he's been gone. You're never seeing him again

Marie Josephine   Oh but I will. I been hearin his drum. You can't keep me locked in here no more. I'm gonna find him.

She starts for her room. **Beartrice** *grabs her.*

Beartrice   You're one crazy roach. Always have been. I had to keep you close most of your life just so you wouldn't lose all of yourself and look at you: ungrateful as a stumped toe.

Marie Josephine   That's 'cause I want to lose myself. That's what love is. Losing it all to make room in your heart for somebody else. When you locked me in that room with no sunlight for seven months I lost him and maybe some of my mind but I ain't never been "fool" moon crazy. That title is reserved for women who kill their men, imprison their daughters and refuse to free their dearest friend. In this regard, big sister, you got my beat by a lifetime.

Beartrice (*to* **Makeda**)   Lock her up.

Makeda *blows the candle out. All goes dark.*

Agnès *and* **Odette** *stop on the porch.*

Agnès   Look at you! Looking like you were born downwind of an outhouse. Ankles exposed like you just come from a womb, breasts sitting out like they holding court, but everybody know they guilty, hair falling off your shoulders like you never brushed up against a comb, and I be damned as the devil if that rouge on your lips is not blood you bit free just so your kiss could kill. You look a whore, Odette. You look like something even a mother couldn't love. Walking round the ball like it's your planet and the rest of us is renting a room. I turned my back on you once and when I looked up you were waltzing with every Harry, Dick and Little Pete from Salkehatchie to Suwannee. Like a trollop. Like a jack-legged Jezabelle. I was so mad I could have ate my face! You were supposed to be acting like you were *maman*. You were supposed to be sitting in the balcony with the other mothers sipping gossip and talking tea. I had to hunt you down twice to get my papers signed and when you finally met Ràmon, you took all night, batting your eyes and smiling your teeth so bright you'd think the lights went out. This was supposed to be my night but you couldn't even stay in costume. You told yourself you were the belle of the ball and you went to town shaking your hips and swinging that tongue, and now I just want to ring your scrawny little neck.

Odette   Oh. You sound upset.

Agnès   Upset?! Upset is a kitten caught up a tree! I'm a big cat and I got my claws *out*!

Odette   Will you hush. Agnès, you'll wake up *Maman* –

Agnès   What I care about waking up *Maman*? I hope she do wake, I hope she come down swinging her cane so I can tell her how whorish you been and maybe she can knock some sense into you. I've never been so embarrassed in all my nineteen years.

Odette   I got hot. I got overwhelmed in all that cloth you stuffed in my dress. My body needed to breathe.

Agnès   Who are you fooling? Them parts was doing more than breathing. They were talking nasty and in French.

Odette   At least my parts do talk. Everything God blessed you with falls flat or sags low. That's why nobody paid you any mind 'cept Ràmon Le Pip and even he looked bored after while. Me: I was toying at least three gents at a time and had them spinning round me like tops.

Agnès   That's 'cause you was masked and nobody got a good look at your face. If they saw how dark you are, they'd run into the night.

Odette   Ràmon got a good look. He seemed to think I was beautiful.

Agnès   You lie.

Odette   *Non*, but that's what he said he wanted to do with me.

Agnès   Liar! Why would he say that?!

Odette   'Cause I let my hair down and he saw the truth. He could tell I wasn't *Maman* even behind the mask. He said my hair was dark as the raven, my skin smooth as the sparrow and when I spoke . . . he said I had the lilt of a lark. He likes birds, Agnès. Did you know that?

Agnès   Course. Course I knew –

Odette   Then you know his favorite is the swan.

Agnès   Course. Course I know his favorite is –

Odette   He said I reminded him of the swan 'cause I move like one when I waltz. I glide on the floor and keep my eyes at my feet. That's when he lifted my chin, took my mask off and said . . . "You are a black swan. The most elegant creature God ever made."

Agnès   Why would he say that? Why would he say that, if he was about to sign my papers?

Odette   He felt obliged to sign, I guess. He said he was sorry he gave you the impression that he liked you when in truth he only liked your body. And *that* till he heard your mouth. He said not much comes out of it and it tires him. I told him you were nervous and that you are warm company . . . when you're asleep. That's when he asked to stay the night with me and sign my papers instead.

Agnès   You wouldn't.

Odette   Course not. I told him no thank you and made him sign yours. I guess if I'm a whore like you say, I'm a really bad one. He signed your papers, you're his *placée*. If I was you, I would never even have come home.

Agnès   I didn't want to, he said he was . . . tired. We're supposed to meet at dawn.

Odette   Well, good for you. Dawn will be here in just a stretch. I'm going upstairs, I promised Maude Lynn I'd untie her before sunrise.

Agnès   Odette? Are you in love with him?

Odette   What kind of question is that? I'm your sister.

Agnès   I know. It's always the ones closest to you that stab you in the back.

Odette *and* **Agnès** *walk inside where* **Beartrice** *is sitting by a single candlelight.*

Beartrice   I'd wish you gals a goodnight. But I can't find nothing good about it yet.

Odette *and* **Agnès**   *Maman?*

Beartrice   Course, *Maman*. What other creature you'd know be up at this hour, sitting in the dark, stroking midnight with her prayers. Every second: an hour of worry, every creep: a jolt of relief for she thinks her children are home – finally. And not raped or wounded or dead and buried in some box.

Agnès   *Maman*, don't be mad. We had to go. We had to make our own way.

Beartrice   I'm too vexed to be mad. Mad is for folks blowing off steam, I'm keeping mine. I'm going to need it to teach y'all this lesson.

She steps forward –

Agnès   It was Odette's idea.

Odette   Liar! You promised to tell the truth.

Agnès   She schemes, *Maman*. She plotted to get us out of the house –

Odette   Agnès, tell the truth!

Agnès   I didn't want to go but she said she could get me placed.

Odette   What I care about her being placed? *Maman*, she made me dress up as you so I could negotiate her price with Ràmon.

Agnès   Look at her! Does she even look like you? She's dressed like a whore. Look at her breasts and her lips, look how she exposes her ankles.

Beartrice Odette, you left my house looking like that?

Odette *Non*, it got hot. Agnès stuffed me, I got hot . . . I couldn't breathe.

Agnès When she walked in the dance hall the men mouths dropped; the mothers fainted as if struck by fever. The servants had to pass round smelling salts just to keep them standing.

Odette She's just jealous! They loved me: the men, the mothers, even the servants. I waltzed all night, I gave them smiles and curtseys. *Maman*, for the first time I was front and center.

Agnès See there, she likes it. She likes playing the whore –

Beartrice Hush, Agnès! Odette Marie Josephine, answer my question. Did you leave my house looking like that?

Odette What difference does it make? I like it. I like me and the way I look. I've spent my whole life in the shadows of you, Agnès, even Maude Lynn, but I've never been seen.

Agnès You were wearing a mask –

Odette I'm not talking 'bout how other folks see me. I'm talking 'bout how *I* see me. In my skin, and I was beautiful. I'm going to bed –

Beartrice Odette, you move a muscle and I'll break a bone. Agnès, give me your papers.

Agnès *retrieves papers.* **Beartrice** *reads.*

Beartrice Just what I was afraid of. Your sister undersold.

Odette Undersold? I got one thousand for her. That's enough money for two whole families to live on for years. Agnès ain't even worth half that.

Beartrice So you know her worth!? You got that wise in the last few hours and can count better than God? This woman's your blood.

Odette She ain't mine! Not no more.

Beartrice *makes her look at* **Agnès**.

Beartrice   *Look at her!* This woman's your flesh! You smart enough to see yourself but can't see the same gal that's been raised beside you all your life. Same gal that wiped your rump, combed your hair for sixteen years, called you favorite. She come from the same womb you spilled from and you still got nerve to put her on the auction block and rope a tag round her neck.

Odette   She wanted it! She wanted to be a *placée*. She didn't care about her price, she just wanted him.

Beartrice   But what did you want for her? You the one sold her. What stock you got in her dreams, in her hopes? What's she worth to you!?

Odette   Not. A. Thing.

Beartrice   Then that's what you sold her for. It's too late for me to save her. Agnès, you belong to Ràmon Le Pip now. But Odette, you still mine. And mine that live in this house will abide by my rules or suffer the consequences. Makeda?!

Makeda *steps into the light.*

Makeda   *Oui, madame.*

Beartrice   Bring the scissors.

Odette   Scissors for what?

Beartrice   For your hair. Your sisters been combing it for sixteen years but now that you sold her, there ain't be nobody round here to keep it combed. So I'm cutting it.

Odette   *Non, Maman,* please . . .

Beartrice   Agnès, hold your sister . . .

Ashamed, **Agnès** *pushes* **Odette** *to her knees.*

Makeda   You don't want to do this, *madame.* A woman's hair is her crown and glory.

Beartrice   I didn't know you had children, Makeda?

Makeda   I don't. But they mine.

She returns to the darkness. She cannot watch.

Beartrice *takes the scissors as* **Agnès** *holds* **Odette**. **Odette** *looks into her mirror (the audience). She will not cry as bunches of her long, glorious hair are cut and fall to the ground.* **Makeda** *won't watch. By the end of the lullaby* **Odette**'s *hair is ear length.*

Maude Lynn (*singing*)
Galine galine galine galo
Galine galine galine galo
Galine galine galo
Galine galine galo

Galo galo mon petit bebe
Galo galo tu vas dormir
Galo galo galo galo
Galine galine galo

Beartrice   A mother's love keeps the balance of nature. (**Odette** *screams as her hair is being cut.*) It can grow any garden; bear any fruit, but it can also burn. (**Odette** *screams.*) If sparked, the same love that nurtures can scorch. (**Odette** *screams.*) To protect, to teach so that new seed can grow.

Beartrice   Makeda, clean up this mess. I need to visit Lazare's wife before sunrise. Now that Agnès is sold, there ain't no reason for me to bring her pie. I'll give her a lump sum from Agnès' purse and keep my house. In the morning, Agnès, I'll go over your papers with you and *Monsieur Le Pip*. He'll pay me six hundred dollars and with the rest we will buy you an apartment on Rampart Street.

Agnès   Six hundred? But *Maman*, that's more than half of my purse.

Beartrice   It's only pennies compared to the real price you'll pay. Odette?

Odette *has turned into ice.*

Beartrice   By the time your hair grows back you will understand why I cut it. Meanwhile, grieve. Your days should be spent mourning your father and not hating me. I'll be back come dawn.

She puts on her shawl and exits through the door. **Le Veuve** *is on the porch.*

La Veuve   I do declare, look who's up with the "going down" moon. Moanin *Madame* Albans.

Beartrice   What you doing out this late, La Veuve? You know it's too early for ugly to be walkin the streets. You makin dogs stray. Go home and cover that insufferable face.

La Veuve   But I am home. I'm going to buy your house. Lazare's widow told me I could get it for cheap since you have no money. Sweet Jesus, when I heard you was poorer than Joe's turkey, I shed a whole tear. I did. That's why I'm really here in fact. I ran over to share it with you. See. See it. It's still in my eye. I'm saving it for you so you can wash the floors with it before I move in.

Beartrice   The only movin you doin is movin them two antsy legs and that wide mouth off my porch. I'm keeping my house. My gal Agnès done tagged the wealthiest man in New Orleans – according to you. So now I'm richer than clabbered cream and got a hop in my step.

La Veuve   What's this? You mean you actually did it? You let one of your gals be placed. What kind of mother are you?

Beartrice   What kind of mother? Woman, pick a face and wear it. Just yester'noon you was telling me I should get them placed before they rot.

La Veuve   Course I did but I was only pulling your bad leg. I hate you, Beartrice, but I don't wish bad thangs upon your daughters. You of all people should know that the day of the *placée* has ended. The fortune you make from your daughter's purse will more than double her pain. Are you willing to sell your gal just so you can pay off Lazare's widow? Is that who you've become, Beartrice Albans? The one person you despise most in this world? A slave trader?!

Time.

Beartrice   It's sad that you hate me so much you'd rather haunt my house in the wee hours of the night than sleep in your own bed, La Veuve. It makes me want to shed a whole tear for you. And I would, if I thought it would wash away your hatefulness but hate is your true love. And one day it will eat you: flesh, bone and sinew till all that is left is your fluttering tongue: that overworked, red cut of meat that for all its flapping, ain't never did nobody no earthly good. (*Beat.*) Have a good morning.

She exits. **La Veuve** *snaps her fan closed. In the parlor,* **Makeda**, *having washed* **Odette**'*s hair, dries it in a towel then braids it.* **Odette** *is barefoot.*

Makeda   It's too hot for you to be going cold on me, Odette. I'd rather see you spit fire, break glass, even scream till you go hoarse than have you curl up into ice. Melt some for Makeda. Ain't you worth at least a tear? You hatin this world now but this feeling is just a winter. If you hold on, spring will blossom a better you and you'll be a woman.

Odette   *Non*, not without my hair. My hair was the best part of me.

Makeda   Your hair was dead. That's what hair is, dead skin.

Odette   I'm not myself without my hair. Look at me. I'm ugly. I'm black and I'm ugly.

Makeda   Come again! Black ain't never been ugly. Half the world's black. And God ain't never made half a mistake. He hung the stars in the black sky because the blackness is brilliant, not the stars. You say you saw yourself at the ball, but you didn't look deep enough. Look now. See yourself this night –

She grabs **Odette**'*s face and forces her to look into the mirror (the audience). In the room:* **Marie** *wakes* **Maude Lynn**.

Marie Josephine   Nite nite, my cry baby. It's time for ya tauntie to fly.

She gets to the door. **Maude Lynn** *wakes.*

Maude Lynn (*half asleep*)   Where you going? It's late, Ta. Go on back to bed.

Marie Josephine   I can't. The moon's falling asleep into the sea. I got to meet my man soon as she lays her head on the river. That's when I'll see him and he'll play his drum for me.

Maude Lynn   Don't try and leave the house. You know *Maman* will have your hide if you do. You should sleep, Ta. We've all had a long day.

Marie Josephine   *Oui*, and a long life for some. This world got all kinds of chains, Maude Lynn. Be one thing when somebody is born in chains, be another when you get chains put on ya. But the saddest in all the world is when you put them chains on yourself. You done chained yourself to a cross that God done already died on, my baby. He don't need you to carry it for the rest of us. God needs you to be you.

Maude Lynn   Listen, you're dreaming, Tauntie. You need to go back to bed.

Marie Josephine   No, I'm not dreaming. Look! There! I see him. (*Beat.*) I'll be seein ya.

Marie Josephine *runs off. Below:* **Makeda** *speaks to* **Odette**.

Makeda   You gone see yourself this night or go blind tryin. LOOK, I SAID!

Odette   I am!

Makeda   Then what you see?

Odette   Nothing. (*Beat. Looks again. She is amazed.*) Nothing but a drum.

Spotlight on a drum. **Marie Josephine** *leaves the house. She runs to Congo Square.*

Makeda
Good. Then you seeing your soul.
You seeing where your blackness began

We hear drumming, it builds.

There. Where Indians carved a square with their feet
    way back when
And danced secrets into the soil that confuse many a
    folk now
For they knew what we will never know:
How to slow a hurry-cane
How to tear loose a tornado
How to grab hold a quake, rock to its beat so as to not
    lose your footing.
Them Indians, God rest 'em,
Was put down long 'fore they brought us round.
Us. We. Kin of Kulekini, cousins of Nkumu
Daughters of Candace
Whose arms we were ripped from and sold.
And souls sold over waters
We came like horses, urged by the whip and was split
No man from the same tribe could mix
This cut into our speech
Made us spit out our mother tongue into the middle
    passage's deep
The only word we kept in our teeth
Was this: MAHALEE! Congo!
From the Mountain Mbanza
Mbanza Kongo Mwene Kabunga
Where our mothers still sit, watchin us from mountain peaks
They told us to find a place where we could speak to them
    with our feet
Dance with the diction of toes into earth
And whatever words we had in our bones so to speak
Could somehow reach and make "beat."
Hear it!
It be the sway in a Negro woman's hip,
The shuffle in a colored man's stride.
The beat be the blackest thang alive
Wake up! See how we survived
Come quick, kin!

Come from every seed and bloodline
Come, you who have only one drop
You who have passed for such a long time
Come, you white as the Lamb
Brown as the furrowed brow
Yellow as teeth
Black as the shadow of an eye
Come you who didn't know you was livin a lie.
Come while the drum is talking some and folks is loose
    and getting loose
Arms spread wide as whales
Wails sung high as moans
Moanin come for long
So put some dance on dem bones
Our mothers throned on peaks have been waiting ever so
(*Wail.*) LOOOOOONG!

The drum goes wild. **Marie Josephine** *arrives at Congo Square.*
She sees the drum. Its beat breaks into her back and she dances, beautifully.

Makeda

Look! Look at her dance before the man who plays the
    bamboulas
Look at her bend her back for his drum
Y'all come look at crazy
She gone make the moon swoon
JESUS! ERZULIE! OSHUN!
Work that beat from your blood
Flood
Dig your feet into this sacred ground
They buried him here
He waited so long
That they put him here
So you could hear his song!

The drumming ends in a final beat. A figure reaches out from the
darkness.

Marie Josephine   Good morning, my love. It's been so
long.

She smiles, runs into the light. It appears that a figure is lifting her into the air. She dances and disappears. In the parlor, **Makeda** *wraps* **Odette***'s hair in an exquisite tignon. Suddenly, a bird whistle.*

Makeda   A bird? Is it dawn already?

Odette   Not yet but soon.

Another bird whistle.

Makeda   That's no bird. Them notes too sharp. What is that?

She peeks past the black curtains.

It's a man out by the fence. Leaning against your mother's palm tree.

Another whistle.

Ooo, he look good enough to eat. He must be that Monsieur Le Pip.

Odette *rushes to the window.*

Odette   Le Pip! Let me see. (*Beat.*) C'est ça. It is him.

Makeda   At least he's early. I better go wake Agnès. If she misses him, she'll be madder than a three-legged dog trying to bury a turd.

She walks upstairs. **Odette** *rushes to the window. She pulls back the curtains and we see the blue before dawn. Time. A figure reaches out to her from the pre-dawn blue. She climbs over the window and exits, barefoot. Time.*

Agnès *and* **Makeda** *come downstairs.* **Agnès** *is dressed in a yellow gown.* **Makeda** *pulls her corset. Enter* **Maude Lynn***.*

Maude Lynn   Where you headed this hour!?

Agnès   Going on a morning stroll with my gentleman. Pull tighter, Makeda. I don't need to breathe.

Maude Lynn   Does *Maman* know?

Agnès   Why? Are you eager to tattle that too? Course, she knows. She's letting me be his *placée*. After all, *Maman* knows best.

She peeks out the window.

Maude Lynn   Makeda, is this true?

Makeda   Mind your own stench, Maude Lynn. And Agnès, don't you and that Pip stray too far. Remember your mother wants you home in a few hours to go over your papers.

Agnès   Where is he? I thought you said he was leaning against the palm tree.

Makeda   He was. Did he climb up it? He seemed pretty eager.

Agnès   I don't see him. (*Calling*) Ràmon!? Ràmon, I'm here.

Makeda   Maybe he went around to the front porch.

She goes to check.

Agnès   Oh, course. Say, Maude Lynn, how do I look?

She curtseys.

Maude Lynn   Peachy and precious. Perfect as ripe plums.

Agnès   Well, that's awful sweet of ya.

Enter **Makeda**.

Makeda   *Non*, he's not out there. Maybe he went round back. Odette should know, she was here.

Agnès   Well, where's Odette?

Makeda   I don't know . . .

Time. Something strikes **Makeda**.

Lord of mercy.

Agnès   What? What is it?

Makeda   Maude Lynn, go see if Odette is in her room.

Maude Lynn *runs upstairs.*

Agnès   Did you leave her alone with him?

Makeda   She wasn't with him, she was just alone.

Agnès   Did she run off with him!? Are they gone?!

Makeda   Don't be rash, she's probably in her room –

Maude Lynn (*calling from downstairs*)   She's not in her room!

Makeda   Jesus.

Agnès   Wait till I get my hands on her! Wait till I get my hands round her neck!

Maude Lynn *enters from downstairs.*

Makeda   Hold on, her shoes are still here. They couldn't have gone far. I'll hurry down the street and catch them. Hold on, Agnès. Maude Lynn, you go check in the servants' quarters.

She grabs the shoes and runs off.

Maude Lynn   Servants' quarters? Why would they be in there?

Makeda   Just go check in the servants' quarters!

Maude Lynn *exits into the back.*

Agnès   I'm going to catch up with them! I'll find them before they get too far!

She exits. **Beartrice** *enters from back.*

Beartrice (*calling upstairs*)   Get up! It's morning! Lord, it's good to be home. Hear that, Lazare? I'm home. Your wife's gonna give me this house for Agnès' papers. Soon as that Monsieur Le Pip gets here and I get my hands in his pockets, these walls will finally be mine. (*Beat.*) Makeda?! Makeda, hurry, I need you.

Enter **Makeda**, *out of breath.*

Makeda   *Oui, madame.*

Beartrice   What are you doing, coming from outside?

Makeda   Odette. We can't find her . . . or Ràmon Le Pip.
I think they run off together.

Beartrice   What you mean, run off?

Enter **Agnès**.

Agnès   They must be halfway cross-town by now.

Enter **Maude Lynn**.

Maude Lynn   Not so . . . I ran into La Veuve sitting in the
park across the street. She said she been there all night and
morning. Said she saw a white man come in the front yard at
dawn, then saw him swing round the house. I went to the slave
quarters to see if Ràmon was there, talking to Odette, and he
was there, but . . .

Beartrice   Go on . . .

Maude Lynn   They wasn't talking . . .

Makeda   Maude Lynn, keep your mouth!

Maude Lynn   He's back there! Rollin round with her!
Naked!

Agnès   Oh, God!

She falls to the ground, trembling.

Beartrice   The gun! Where's my gun?

Makeda   Don't do it, *madame*.

Beartrice *rushes out back.*

Agnès   She's not leaving here with him! She's brought shame
on this house! If I don't get him neither should she. What she
got that I don't have? What's in her blood that ain't in mine?

A shot!

Ràmon? Dear God . . . Ràmon?!

Maude Lynn   Merciful Savior!

Makeda   See what a sharp tongue can wrought, Maude Lynn. Now the whole family bleeds.

Maude Lynn   But I was trying to save them. I was . . . I . . .

Enter **Beartrice** *with gun.*

Agnès   *Maman,* you killed him?

Beartrice   Not even close. Though God knows I tried to take his head off. Shoulda known I'd be no good with guns. I merely scrapped his ear. He jumped up, grabbed Odette and they ran off, both of them naked as jaybirds.

Maude Lynn   She's never coming back now. We'll never see her again.

Beartrice   Don't matter. She's dead to me. And nobody is to talk 'bout her again. *Ecoute-moi?* She's dead! Don't even let her name walk 'cross your lips. We will mourn her like proper free colored women. In silence. Dressed in our best black.

Agnès   But what about me? Ràmon was my last chance. Look at me! (*To God.*) Look at this. God! Look at what you made! This body! You're gonna let all of this – ? All of this be lonely?

Maude Lynn   Come now, sis, you're not alone –

She takes her sister's hand.

Agnès   I'm old! Aged in minutes. I didn't get out fast enough and now look. I look like – (*To* **Beartrice**.) you. This is what you wanted, isn't it? *Maman?* May I have my papers, please?

Beartrice *hands her the document.*

Agnès   There be no need for these.

She rips her papers. She is frozen.

Makeda   *Non*, Agnès! That was to pay off the house. Your purse was the only fortune we had.

Beartrice   Don't matter, he'd cut her off anyway. I'm just
going to have to make do. I'm going to have to go back there
and give that woman what she wants.

Makeda   I can't let you do that, *madame.*

Beartrice   Ain't got no choice. If I hurry, she might be in a
better mood. She gets testy by midday.

She starts to exit.

Makeda   *Non, madame.*

*She unwraps her head scarf and reveals the king's ransom she's been
hiding on her head: silver, gold coins, jewelry she got from* **La Veuve**,
bills, a diamond, pearls and a gold-plated brooch.

Makeda   I was saving this for a rainy day but . . . God's
been cryin on us enough. Here. Give it to the wife. It should
be just enough to keep the house.

Beartrice   You know I don't take things for free, Makeda –

Makeda   I know. Be why it's not for free. This for my freedom.

Time.

Beartrice   I see. Course. (*Beat.*) Well . . . fair 'nough. Maude
Lynn, bring me my ink and blotter.

She retrieves papers, seals and signs. She hands them to **Makeda** *and
offers a shake.* **Makeda** *holds* **Beartrice**'s *hand in hers and kisses
them.* **Makeda** *reads:*

Makeda (*reading with a bit of struggle at first*)
　　Know all men by these presents . . .
　　That Makeda Albans (a God-fearing Negro woman)
　　Of the City of New Orleans
　　For divers good and sufficient sacrifice
　　Causes me thereunto . . . moving have manumitted
　　Emancipated . . . set free from slavery

Beartrice
　　For a sum no man can number

And only a woman can gather
She: has freed herself. And served us
As sister, mother, nurturer . . . and dearest friend.

Makeda *holds back tears.*

Makeda
She is to work and gain sufficient livelihood for herself
With her wisdom and charity, she shall be a beacon
For generations.

Beartrice
Even after this tattered paper fades and history books
    erase her
She shall still be the foundation
Of a nation that was raised by her hand
It is the strength she buried in us
That will carry us through
/ I have set my seal hereunto

Makeda
I have set my seal hereunto. This day:
The fourth day of July anno domini – 1836 . . .
 Beartrice Albans.

She gets her traveling bag and heads into the audience.

(*Singing, slow at first.*) Jordan river, you can't help me cross.

When she opens the door, dawn, in her full glory rushes in. It floods the house.

Maud Lynn's *last moment which completes her arch.*

Beartrice   Well, would you look at that. Dawn has finally lifted her skirt. It's morning. So let us mourn. We shall start with early-day prayers and supplication, light tea, then elocution lessons in Latin, noonday prayer, embroidery, then sitting with your father's body . . . Agnès, Maude Lynn, go fetch your veils.

Agnès   *Oui, maman.*

She gets her veil, **Maude Lynn** *does not move.*

Maude Lynn   *Non. Non.* I'm done with mourning the dead. I want to live!

She hurries to the door.

Beartrice   MAUDE LYNN!

Maude Lynn *freezes.*

Maude Lynn   *Oui, Maman.*

Beartrice   Don't you dare take another step. The Bible says honor thy mother, which is the first commandment with promise!

Maude Lynn   *Oui.* But it also say that every man seek his own soul's salvation.

With all the courage she can muster, **Maude Lynn** *steps out of the house and exhales!*

Beartrice   Maude Lynne Therese!

Maud Lynn *walks away.*

Makeda (*singing offstage*)
   I got one more river to cross.

Time. **Beartrice** *sits.* **Agnès** *enters and sits.*

Beartrice (*to* **Anges**) Figures! Them hags wasn't as tough as us. They didn't have the teeth to cut life nor the sense to know how truly free they were, locked in here livin in the lap of God. It's a devil's scheme.

Makeda (*softly*)
   Jordan river, you can't help me cross.

Makeda *hums.* **Agnès** *covers her face with the veil.*

Beartrice (*to the audience*)   They'll be gone three days and their stomachs will growl and eat away at their bellies. Their tongues will dry like cracked feet as they thirst for the milk of my tears.

Makeda
> Only I can get me across,
> Not my mother, not my brother –

Makeda *hums.*

Beartrice   This hateful world will claw into their backs and plant bitter crop between their legs, boiling their eggs into hard-headed children. Men will dance on their hearts, breaking them into chunks of flesh and gambling away the pieces for half pennies and hog parts. They'll be spat on because of the color of their skin. Raped 'cause of their flesh. Made to slave in kitchens 'cause of their sex. Oh, you hate me now. But age will teach you how great was my love. And when you come back, crawling on your necks, begging me with your baby eyes . . . I'll still be here, sitting on my throne. I'll sit back . . . suck my teeth and say . . . so sweetly . . .

She finally breaks, weeps tears.

Well . . . welcome home.

Darkness swallows the women.

Makeda
> I got one more river
> One more river to cross!

As lights fade, in shadow, **Lazare** *passes by, staring at* **Beartrice**.

Blackout.

Glossary

adieu – means "see you." This one is tricky. Pronounced ***ah-do'ye***

bamboulas – a type of drum and dance from Africa. Pronounced ***bam-boo-lahs***

bon – means good. Pronounced with pop: ***b[o]n***

calinda – an African dance. Pronounced ***ka-linda***

calotte – means funeral hat. Pronounced ***cuh-lot***

chapeau – means hat. Pronounced ***sha-po***

cher – means dear. Pronounced ***share***

coiffure – means hairdresser. Pronounced ***cwa-fur***

ga line – means "watch the moon." Pronounced ***gah-leen***

ga lo – means "watch the water." Pronounced ***gah-low***

je promesse – means "I promise." Pronounced ***juh-pro-mess***

les anges – means angels. Pronounced ***leys-ahn'je***

ma maison – means "my house." Pronounced ***ma-may-zon***

maître – means master. Pronounced ***may-truh***

mam'zelle – means miss, short for mademoiselle in French. Pronounced ***ma'am-zell***

Marseille – a city in France. Pronounced ***mar-say-yuh***

merci, Dieu merci – means thank God. Pronounced ***mer-see***

mes filles – means "my daughters." This one is tricky, it's pronounced ***may-fee-yuhs*** or ***may-fee***

mo chagren ma chère – means "I'm sorry my dear." Pronounced ***mo-sha-gin-ma-share***

pauvre – means poor, as in sad, not impoverished. Pronounced ***po-vrah***

plaçage – the system of concubibinge between free women of color and white men who were in common-law marriages with them. Pronounced ***pluh-sage***

placée – means woman, usually a quadroon who is part of the concubinage system of *plaçage*. Pronounced ***plah-say***

repose en paix mon père – means "rest in peace my father." Pronounced ***reh-pose-awn-pay-mawn-pear***

salut – means hello. Pronounced ***sah-loo***

selas or *selah* – means Selah, praise or meditation in the
   Bible. Pronounced **say-la**

silence – means silence. Pronounced (not at all as in English)
   see-lawnce

Tauntie – means auntie. Pronounced **taunt-tee**

très jolie – means very pretty. Pronounced **tray-jo-lee**

tu vas dormir – means go to sleep. Pronounced **too-vah-dor-
   meer**

Vacherie – a plantation area outside New Orleans.
   Pronounced **vah-shuh-ree**

  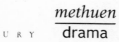 

Bloomsbury Methuen Drama Modern Plays
include work by

Bola Agbaje
Edward Albee
Davey Anderson
Jean Anouilh
John Arden
Peter Barnes
Sebastian Barry
Alistair Beaton
Brendan Behan
Edward Bond
William Boyd
Bertolt Brecht
Howard Brenton
Amelia Bullmore
Anthony Burgess
Leo Butler
Jim Cartwright
Lolita Chakrabarti
Caryl Churchill
Lucinda Coxon
Curious Directive
Nick Darke
Shelagh Delaney
Ishy Din
Claire Dowie
David Edgar
David Eldridge
Dario Fo
Michael Frayn
John Godber
Paul Godfrey
James Graham
David Greig
John Guare
Mark Haddon
Peter Handke
David Harrower
Jonathan Harvey
Iain Heggie

Robert Holman
Caroline Horton
Terry Johnson
Sarah Kane
Barrie Keeffe
Doug Lucie
Anders Lustgarten
David Mamet
Patrick Marber
Martin McDonagh
Arthur Miller
D. C. Moore
Tom Murphy
Phyllis Nagy
Anthony Neilson
Peter Nichols
Joe Orton
Joe Penhall
Luigi Pirandello
Stephen Poliakoff
Lucy Prebble
Peter Quilter
Mark Ravenhill
Philip Ridley
Willy Russell
Jean-Paul Sartre
Sam Shepard
Martin Sherman
Wole Soyinka
Simon Stephens
Peter Straughan
Kate Tempest
Theatre Workshop
Judy Upton
Timberlake Wertenbaker
Roy Williams
Snoo Wilson
Frances Ya-Chu Cowhig
Benjamin Zephaniah

For a complete listing of Bloomsbury
Methuen Drama titles, visit:
www.bloomsbury.com/drama

Follow us on Twitter and keep up to date
with our news and publications
@MethuenDrama